From the Pages of *Forget Self-Help*

"Nonetheless, when someone bears our burdens with us, often a huge weight lifts from our shoulders. Does this mean that the other person can solve the problem that the other one is going through? *No.* However, just knowing that someone cares enough to forget his *own* problems and focus on *yours* is reassuring."

—CHAPTER 1

"When people speak of having an advantage over someone, they often feel as if they have to tread on sharp glass. There is no need to do this because none of us created our own advantages. They were given to us. However, we do need to tread lightly on how we use our own advantages to help others." —CHAPTER 2

"Usually, when we ourselves are in a position or power, we like to look to see how we can use it to control others instead of realizing that we need to control ourselves that much more because of the position we are now in." —CHAPTER 2

"A man's heart is only strong when it is safe, and it is only safe when it is secured in something strong." —CHAPTER 2

"Since none of us will see God on Earth, we face an uphill battle to show others that God truly exists." —CHAPTER 3

"One reason that we never get to know other people is because it requires us to become vulnerable to other people. To become vulnerable not only requires work ... y people are unwilling to admit their ... when this happens, a whole new world is opened up because it enables both parties to be real with each other." —CHAPTER 4

"Without loving oneself first, it is impossible to love others." —CHAPTER 4

"Everyone can agree though that anything worthwhile, anything worth striving for, has some element of rarity to it." —CHAPTER 5

"When judging another person, I never look for the big moments that test their character. I look for the small ones. Big moments carry a heroic aspect to them so there is a certain selfish incentive to make sure they are carried out to fruition. Small moments, however, never get any credit. This accentuates their value." —CHAPTER 6

"We need to be extreme, we need to be bold, we need to go all out, but we need to do this all for others, not ourselves." —CHAPTER 6

"The best way to tell if someone is with you is to see whether a person will help you even if he knows he will get nothing in return from you. Anyone can help when there is something to gain in return; to help when there is nothing to be gained shows true love." —CHAPTER 7

"Showing mercy toward others is not an easy task. It requires patience, humility, and an inverse style of thinking that goes against our natural selfish desires. It also requires giving up a sense of control, a sense of control we often feel like we earned in the first place.." —CHAPTER 7

2

"Holding someone accountable for their actions can be one of the most delicate and awkward dealing that a human being has to do for another. But in strong relationships, this happens frequently." —CHAPTER 8

"So many times, we lash out against others when they give us advice or critique our actions. We need to realize they are doing so because they believe in us and think we are capable of greatness." —CHAPTER 8

"When we do for others, we provide more happiness for ourselves more effectively than when we try to focus only on ourselves. The reason for this is simple: putting ourselves in another's shoes makes us forget all about our own problems." —CHAPTER 8

"What happens when we focus less on ourselves and instead devote that energy toward others? We benefit others and also benefit ourselves. When we reach out to someone who is in need, we fulfill the words of Christ. By following the Golden Rule in our attitude, behavior, and conduct, we make the world a better place and make our own lives better too." —CHAPTER 9

"You only love someone when you are willing to sacrifice for them; without sacrifice, there is no love." —CHAPTER 9

Forget Self-Help

Re-Examining the Golden Rule

Thomas Fellows

Forget Self-Help
Re-Examining the Golden Rule

© 2017 Thomas Fellows

ISBN 978-0-9984606-7-3

BORGO
PUBLISHING

www.borgopublishing.com
205.454.4256

First Edition

Cover design by Easty Lambert-Brown

Printed in the United States of America

CONTENTS

INTRODUCTION

The main thesis of this book is simple: the best way to help yourself is to help others. I don't consider myself to be an accomplished literary scholar, a historian, a psychiatrist, or theologian, but I have battled clinical depression for nearly a decade which has lead me to gain certain insights. I have known what brings me the most joy and what leaves me feeling the most depleted; I wrote the book so you, the reader, would be able to share in the insights I have gained.

My secondary thesis is that the words that Jesus encourages us to live out in Matthew 7:12 when he says, "so in everything, do to others what you would have them do to you, for this sums up the law and prophets" is almost forgotten by the church today. The reason why I believe this is a forgotten part about Christianity is because in all my dealings growing up with going to church, attending Bible studies, hearing lectures, etc., this verse was rarely if ever mentioned. Additionally, many of the Christians that I know in my life today never seem to pay attention to this Golden Rule as it is called, (myself included.)

At no other time in the Bible does Jesus remark, "for this sums up the law and prophets" as he does in Matthew 7:12.

Luckily, I had one mentor who was different: Scoot Dimon of The Westminster Schools. He encouraged us students to live out the words of Jesus when he tells his disciples to "go and do likewise" in Luke 10:37 after Jesus tells the story of The Good Samaritan. Mr. Dimon reminding me of that teaching has been one of the most important avenues to strengthen my faith in Him.

*

I am from Atlanta, GA, but spent considerable time in Alabama for college at Samford University in Birmingham and at Camp Laney in Mentone, AL during the summer. I started writing this book over 7 years ago during the summer of 2010 in Mentone, AL at age 21. I love The South, I enjoy literature and I appreciate studying prominent historical figures. The book deals with four subjects: two literary and two historical, all four Southern in nature.

The first subject is Harper Lee's, *To Kill a Mockingbird*. It was published in 1960. It has been named the best novel of the 20th century and in a survey taken in 2006 in which a group of librarians were asked which book should someone read before they die, it beat out The Bible for the number one spot. For the past few years, I have given away the book as baby presents for close friends that have recently had a child because the parenting style of Atticus is one to be modeled after.

Uncle Tom's Cabin, by Harriet Beecher Stowe, was published in 1852. It sold over 300,000 copies the first year. It is famously noted that when Abraham Lincoln ran into Harriet Beecher Stowe for the first time he allegedly remarked, "So you're the little woman who wrote the book that started this great war!"

Robert E. Lee is widely considered the greatest military strategist of all time. Even though at he went to West Point, he commanded the Confederate Army against The United States. He fought for the South because he refused to fight against his family. It should be noted that in a letter addressing his stance on slavery dated December 27, 1856, "There are few, I believe, in this enlightened age, who will not acknowledge that slavery as an institution is a moral and political evil. It is idle to expatiate on its disadvantages. I think it is a greater evil to the white than to the colored race." Additionally, Lee wrote in a letter to his son, "But I can anticipate no greater calamity for the country than a dissolution of the Union. It would be an accumulation of all the evils we complain of, and I am willing to sacrifice everything but honor for its preservation. I hope, therefore, that all constitutional means will be exhausted before there is a resort to force. Secession is nothing but revolution." What's a little-known fact to the general public is that Abraham Lincoln wanted the black race to be shipped back to Africa while Lee wanted them to stay. Reading Lee's quotes during my first bout with depression eased my pain and strengthened my faith greatly.

Martin Luther King Jr. is arguably considered to be the most influential American ever to live and is the only American to have a holiday named after him. That holiday was signed into law by President Ronald Reagan in 1983. With his eloquent words, nonviolent resistance and strong reason, he was able to grant African-American civil rights once and for all. I am proud to be forever linked to MLK Jr. through my work I am doing at Morehouse College coaching their Competition Sales Team. He enrolled at Morehouse when he was 15 years-old and graduated from there in 1948.

Both Robert E. Lee and Martin Luther King Jr. shared a common thread that some may say helped lead to their empathetic nature: clinical depression.

*

Malcom Gladwell once said, "good writing does not succeed or fail on the strength of its ability to persuade. It succeeds or fails on the strength of its ability to engage you, to make you think, to give you a glimpse into someone else's head." I hope I achieved this throughout the pages of *Forget Self-Help*.

ACKNOWLEDGEMENTS

Growing up, I attended The Westminster Schools in Atlanta, GA; English was my favorite subject. I was first introduced to *To Kill a Mockingbird* by Harper Lee in 6th grade by Chuck Breithaupt when we read a chapter of the book and saw the movie. I read it for the first time in 9th grade with Catherine Nelson and it soon became my favorite book of all time.

I would reap the benefits by having three other fine English teachers at Westminster in high school. Tiffany Boozer taught me two classes. What impressed me so much about her is that she quit her job at arguably the most prestigious law firm in the South, King and Spalding, to go teach. Her undergrad degree came from UVA and she got her JD at UGA. Thad Persons taught me Junior Year. He went to Princeton for Undergrad and got his Masters in teaching at Columbia. As my sales career has progressed, I've realized how much financial success he could have had if he had entered the corporate world instead of teaching. My final teacher that I had was Jennifer Dracos. Her creative writing course would teach me that it was not only okay to think outside of the box, but that great writing did this. She turned down a lucrative writing career at a consulting company after going to Brown to go teach. It is easy to see the common theme throughout this paragraph: all sacrificed monetary gain to grow and shape the minds of young students.

In 10th grade, I had a history teacher who would go on to be one of the most influential people in my life. The book wouldn't exist had it not been for him. His name is Joe Tribble and he suggested that I read *Uncle Tom's Cabin*, by Harriet Beecher Stowe. I obliged and soon almost had to choose it as my favorite book over *To Kill a Mockingbird*. Mr. Tribble also taught me about Robert E. Lee and Martin Luther King Jr. in his U.S. History class.

I want to also thank Jenna Buckley, a classmate of mine from Westminster who encouraged me during a time of deep distress in December of 2016.

I want to also thank my psychiatrist Dr. Lyndon Waugh. He has aided me greatly during these past five years of treatment and was a great influence during the past few months giving me advice on the publishing process. He is author of best-seller *Tired of Yelling*.

I want to also thank Steve Mitby of AZA Law Firm in Houston.

I want to also thank John Grisham who is my favorite fiction writer of all time. His novels *The Last Juror* and *Camino Island* assisted me greatly in this endeavor.

I want to also thank Malcom Gladwell who is my favorite non-fiction writer. I hope I learned from his works to think outside of the box like he does.

I want to also thank Kay Redfield Jamison: I can only hope that this book proved her point.

I want to thank Easty Lambert-Brown of Borgo Publishing for all her help in this process and her honesty.

One of the reasons I finished this book is because of one of my best friends, the late Nick Pinkerton. Nick tragically took his life in 2014, but not before being one of the first people to read some of my work. He encouraged me to finish it. If anyone understood how to live out the Golden Rule, it was Nick, and everyone around him knew that.

QUOTES FROM EACH SUBJECT ON THE GOLDEN RULE

Matthew 7:12. "So in everything, do to others what you would have them do to you, for this sums up the Law and the Prophets."
—*Holy Bible* NIV

"We does for the Lord when we does for his critturs,"
—Tom, *Uncle Tom's Cabin*

"First of all," he said, "if you can learn a simple trick, Scout, you'll get along a lot better with all kinds of folks. You never really understand a person until you consider things from his point of view [...] until you climb into his skin and walk around in it."
—Atticus, *To Kill a Mockingbird*

"Life's most persistent and urgent question is, what are you doing for others?"
—Martin Luther King Jr.

"Teach him he must deny himself."
—When a woman asked Robert E. Lee to bless his son

"The best possible thing you can do is to forget yourself."
—TIM KELLER

1

Crying for Someone Other Than Yourself

What happens when we focus less on ourselves and instead devote that energy toward others? Put in a different light, what happens when we start helping others rather than ourselves? What happens is an amazing contradiction, which in economics is known as "interdependent utility function," meaning that your *own* happiness is based upon *others'* happiness. This way of thinking can be seen frequently by individuals' actions mentioned throughout this book. In order to possess interdependent utility function, you might think that you have to be a gifted individual who has never had setbacks so that you can pass off only positive energy to another … *wrong*! The more challenges you have had to overcome, the more confident you will be because those trying experiences will help you to help others. Not only that, but it will allow you to cry for others even more because you have been in that experience … certainly an odd way to look at your own troubles.[1]

---

[1] In December 2016, I had a gut-wrenching acute 48-hour depression, the worst of my life. Ultimately, what got me through it was not complaining about it, but instead thanking God for the strife because it would make me

There is nothing as powerful as for a human being to cry for another human being. It is natural for people to cry. Whether it is failing to get the lead in the high school play, realizing you have graduated from a size six to a size eight, or losing your once secure career in this economy, we all have reason to cry sometimes. Or do we? Crying for others rather than for oneself is one of the most irrational, strange, and uncommon things for a person to do. It goes against what we believe life is all about. However, a quick glimpse into one's own life reveals the secret to living a joyful one. The secret does not focus on you necessarily, but on others.

When someone receives a sorrow, we must remember that the effect is exponential in its power to transform. One great instance of this is shown in a beautiful scene of *Uncle Tom's Cabin; or, Life among the Lowly,* by Harriet Beecher Stowe.

This scene takes place in the famous cabin of Uncle Tom for whom the book is named. Tom's wife, Chloe, has just found out that the Shelby's plan is to sell Tom, the noble humble Christian slave who did everything he could do to help out on the plantation and was promised his freedom. The Shelby's had been seen as being kind, relatively speaking, to their slaves. In fact, Mrs. Shelby often repeatedly talked to her husband about freeing all of the slaves. This was brought about by one thing: her Christlike nature.

The day Tom was set to leave the plantation, one of Chloe's boys called out to his mother to tell her that Mrs. Shelby was coming in to the cabin. Not surprisingly, Chloe answered, "She can't do no good, what's she coming for." That is a natural response that anyone might have in any sort of crisis.

---

have that much more empathy for people because I had been through so much pain myself.

Anyone can become an enemy, and often times we lash out at the messenger or someone who is trying to help us. Nonetheless, when someone bears our burdens with us, often a huge weight lifts from our shoulders. Does this mean that the other person can solve the problem that the other one is going through? *No*. However, just knowing that someone cares enough to forget his *own* problems and focus on *yours* is reassuring. I know that, deep down, God loves each one of us and has sacrificed his Son for each of us. In the moment of that clinging depression, however, does that realization even help? Ultimately it can help and has helped me before, but I have been alive on this earth for 28 years and have *never* seen God in the flesh. God has never given me an encouraging word or given me a pat on the back the way a grandfather can. Because we will never see God on Earth, we are called to be God's agents here on Earth, which happens later in the passage.

Mrs. Shelby entered. Aunt Chloe set a chair for her in a manner decidedly gruff and crusty. She did not seem to notice either the action or manner. She looked pale and anxious.

"Tom," she said, "I come to—" and stopping suddenly, and regarding the silent group, she sat down in the chair, and, covering her face with her handkerchief, began to sob.

"Lor, now, Missis, don't—don't" said Aunt Chloe, bursting out in her turn; and for a few moments all wept in company. And in those tears they all shared together, the high and the lowly, melted away all the heart- burnings and anger of the oppressed. O, ye who visit the distressed do ye know that everything your money can buy, given with a cold averted face, is not worth one honest tear shed in real sympathy.

Compare Aunt Chloe's initial mood to her feeling when another cries her heart out with what Chloe is going through. Substituting Mrs. Shelby's feelings and gestures for Aunt Chloe's shows how much Mrs. Shelby cares. Mrs. Shelby's first action is very uncommon to her: she ignores what Aunt Chloe has done for her. Chloe's reaction seems normal considering what she was going through. The narrator then describes Mrs. Shelby as "pale and anxious," again, words that could easily describe Chloe's mood but a bit of a surprising description of a slave owner's wife's mood for the situation. In the next *vulnerable* and *powerful* action, Mrs. Shelby tries to give a powerful sending off before breaking down in tears.

In the South, in that time period, it would have been a rare sight to see a white person cry for another black person's emotions, due to the fact that many white people did not believe black people even capable of emotions, so of course they saw no need to tip-toe around them. This action by Mrs. Shelby is so poignant because of what it does to Aunt Chloe: Chloe goes from not wanting to speak to Mrs. Shelby to being the one who consoles Mrs. Shelby.

*

There is no greater way to ease someone else's emotion than to feel it yourself. This rarely happens because human beings are programmed to care only about their own emotions. Society tells us to care about our own emotions, in part, because many times society only wants to make money off of us. For instance, did you know that *Listerine* virtually invented bad breath with marketing ploys? As scholar Cecil Munsey states in his writing "Often a Bridesmaid but never a Bride", "as a mouthwash it wasn't a runaway success until the 1920s, when it was pitched as a solution for "chronic halitosis." According to advertising scholar James Twitchell, "Listerine did not make mouthwash as much as it made halitosis. In just seven years, because of its supposed "triumph" over bad breath, the company's revenues rose from $115,000 to more than $8 million." We are taught and even encouraged to make sure we do our best to care about ourselves, making us often forget to do that which brings us the most joy and purpose: to care for others.

It is a rare occurrence to see someone act this way, but its impact on humanity is monumental. Taking a quick glimpse into Chloe's heart after it was made soft illustrates this perfectly: "'Lor, now, Missis, don't—don't!' said Aunt Chloe, bursting out in her turn, and for a few moments they all wept in company. And in those tears they all shed together, the high and the lowly, melted away all the heart-burnings and anger of the oppressed."

Both ladies act how they do because of the belief and faith in something more purposeful than each trying to make themselves *happy* all the time. Their counter-intuitive actions arose from their belief in encouragement from scripture such as these words found in Galatians 6:2: "Carry each other's burdens, and in this way you will fulfill the law of Christ."

In this specific instance Mrs. Shelby's actions, at least in the short term, swiftly and abruptly dispelled disaster. Oftentimes, people have preconceived notions about their fellow beings that lead them to distrust. Naturally, when somebody goes out of their way to do something thoughtful, it might surprise us, maybe even shock us.

There is no greater feeling to be shocked for the right reasons. So many times in life we are shocked for the wrong reasons. You might be shocked by being cutoff in traffic. You might be shocked that a person talked behind your back after you had avidly stuck up for him in the past. You might be shocked that a person is jealous of you for achieving success even after you fought a hard, long path.

I would argue as tough as those situations are, we can eventually forget them. One thing that we cannot forget is when someone shocks us for the right reasons.

In *To Kill a Mockingbird*, by Harper Lee, Tom Robinson, a black man, is wrongly accused of raping Mayella Ewell, a white woman. Atticus Finch, Scout and Jem's father, is appointed to try the near-impossible case in an old southern town called Maycomb, Alabama.

During a critical time in the trial after a clear-cut racist act occurs, Dill—Scout and Jem's best friend—leaves the courtroom because he cannot stand the injustice in the courtroom. He feels the pain, anger, and sorrow so strongly that it upsets his stomach, the way you feel when *you* have been wronged. Just like it is a miracle for Mrs. Shelby to feel emotion for Aunt Chloe, it is also a miracle for Dill to feel any emotion for what is happening in that courtroom.

Dolphus Raymond, known as the town drunk and seen as an outcast because he proudly and gladly associates with black people, is pleasantly surprised when he sees Dill feeling a little bit dizzy, and in that dizziness he did not see weakness, but strength. To ease his pain Dolphus offers him a sip of his drink, which everyone thinks is Coca-Cola mixed with a little bit of alcohol. To Dill's surprise, when he sips the drink, it is just plain Coca-Cola. All of this makes Scout wonder why Dolphus tricks everyone in this way. Raymond explains he does so that people will not think he is crazy for hanging around black people.

Before going any further to the main point, taking a deeper look into Raymond's actions reveals how muddled the town of Maycomb is. However, rather than demonizing Maycomb, the Old South, and white people in general, we must realize that this type of scene happens daily in our own everyday lives.

Needless to say, we're often weary of what people think about us, but Luke 6:26 tells us "woe to you when all men speak well of you." Raymond seems to take this to heart, but only to an extent; he realizes the frailty of human condition because the town needs something to help them understand his choice to hang around black people.

Either way, the children are entrusted with this dark secret, and curious Scout asks why they have the privilege and honor of knowing. Raymond's answer is simple: because Dill has the *heart* to cry. Dill was not crying because he failed to get his favorite candy at the grocery store. Dill wasn't crying because he thought he was wronged by some kids who were bullying him. No, he was crying because there was *another* man being bullied, who he didn't even know; or, did he actually know Tom Robinson better than anyone because he had the heart to cry for him?

Dill's cry for justice encourages Raymond to tell these children his secret. He is thrilled to have someone to talk to about it, a person who is enlightened or unenlightened, depending on who you ask. He goes on to tell them: "Things haven't caught up with that one's instinct yet. Let him get a little old … and he won't get sick and cry. Maybe things'll strike him as being—not quite right, say, but he won't cry, not when he gets a few years on him."

Crying is often seen as weak. Often, society tells us that if we are sad, then there is something wrong with us. Sometimes, we are told that in order to combat this sadness, we have to buy this gadget or that one. However, Dill's sadness could not be consoled that way because it was society that caused it. He was "crying about the simple hell people give other people—without even thinking." He deserves an immense amount of respect. It's easy to see why Raymond was so moved by the little boy. When a society or group of people sees a person with true sadness against its principles, it stiffens up and reacts in a way that causes even more heartache for that person.

In my life when I have gotten depressed, I immediately grow more selfish than I already am. When you are depressed, you try whatever means you have to in order to dig yourself out of the hole you are in. One of the symptoms of depression is irritability. We are mad at the world, mad at other people, mad at the situation we find ourselves in. What we do not realize, however. is that the more we try to dig ourselves out of a hole, the deeper the hole we dig. We were not put on this earth just to make ourselves happy. We were put on this earth to care for others.

*

One example of me crying for another human occurred in 2014 when my best friend's brother reached out to me because one of his best friends at University of Georgia was going through a similar situation as I went through when I was at the University of Alabama when I was diagnosed with bipolar disorder. The young man was having a manic episode and needed help fast. I was in Atlanta at the time and had just finished a day of cold calling. When I heard he was in trouble, I knew I had no choice but to drive up to Athens and go help him out. We met at Little Italy in Athens. I thought he was showing clear signs of mania so I got him to the nearest local hospital. I stayed up with him until the wee hours of the morning in the hospital to make sure everything was okay. While some may have seen this as an inconvenience, I did not. I couldn't have called myself a Christian if I hadn't followed through with it. After all, Robert E. Lee once said, "Duty then is the sublimest word in the English language. You should do your duty in all things. You can never do more, you should never wish to do less."

*

There is nothing more a human seeks than to have intimacy with another human. It could be a romantic relationship, it could be a mentor-mentee relationship, or it could be a simple friendship. Intimacy involves loving one another. Loving one another means that your happiness is based upon the other person's happiness and vice-versa. Intimacy is wonderful, but it takes time and effort and is very taxing on one's heart. More than anything, it takes risk. It takes risking your feelings, risking taking the time and effort to have intimacy, risking the chance of being hurt. Intimacy is not one's desire to have money, power, and so on. We cannot have intimacy with another person until we give up these trivial things. Only when we give up these trivial things do we have the chance to get intimate with another human being. Oftentimes, once we feel intimate with another, it leads us to change our hearts to come back for more.

*

Many times, we will choose to cry for some people but not others. Oftentimes, our subconscious chooses whom we help because we know they can pay us back a favor. In other words, when people of high status act kind toward "lower status" parties, it is rare and surprises people like Mr. Raymond because this action goes directly against survival of the fittest instinct and a natural response to incentives.

An example of this can be found in Robert E. Lee's own life. Lee was not your typical leader of today: if he wanted something done that was risky and dangerous, he would prefer to do it himself. One day when Lee was in battle, he called his men to come back to where he was to get out of harm's way, or so it appeared. As soon as his men followed orders, he himself went to the clump of trees where the men had just been. His bewildered men wondered why he would do such a thing. Nonetheless, it was all worth it for Lee because there was a baby bird on the ground that needed to be put back in one of those trees. It was an act that no man would feel comfortable doing because it was beneath him, but it was not beneath Lee.

*

Robert E. Lee put it best when he said, "I cannot consent to place in the control of others one who cannot control himself." In *To Kill a Mockingbird*, Scout wonders why Atticus even takes the case of Tom Robinson in the first place:

"If you shouldn't be defending him, then why are you doin' it?"

"For a number of reasons," said Atticus, "The main one is, if I didn't I couldn't hold up my head in town, I couldn't represent this country in the legislature, I couldn't even tell you or Jem not to do something again."

"Atticus, are we going to win it?"

"No, honey."

"Then why—"

"Simply because we were licked a hundred years before we started is no reason for us not to try and win," Atticus said.

What if leadership in our churches, our schools, our government, and our business ran this way? We would have less trouble, fewer lawsuits, and we could trust one another for a change. When organizations hold themselves to the highest standard from the very top, they prosper. Unfortunately, many people don't want to shoulder that responsibility.

Who are the baby birds who have fallen from the tree in our own lives? Is it the arrogant coworker who needs someone to reassure him that he is a valued member of the team and his opinions do matter? Is it the high school student who gets bullied constantly because of a speech impediment? Or maybe it is yourself, who feels as though you are the only person who reaches out to people and no one ever reaches back out to you. It is impossible for the baby bird to get back into the tree without the help of someone like Robert E. Lee in this instance.

*

In another scene in *Uncle Tom's Cabin,* an equally poignant scene plays out with a senator from Ohio and his wife. At first, both Sen. John Bird and his wife, Mary, are debating whether they think a recent law that passed is the right one. The law decrees that it is unlawful to aid and abet slaves coming from Kentucky. Mary knows her husband well enough to know that he wouldn't turn away a runaway slave that needed help:

"O, nonsense, John! you can talk all night, but you wouldn't do it. I put it to you, John,—would you now turn away a poor, shivering, hungry creature from your door, because he was a runaway? Would you, now?"

Now, if the truth must be told, our senator had the misfortune to be a man who had a particularly humane and accessible nature, and turning away anybody that was in trouble never had been his forte; and what was worse for him in this particular pinch of the argument was, that his wife knew it, and, of course was making an assault on rather an indefensible point. So he had recourse to the usual means of gaining time for such cases made and provided; he said "ahem," and coughed several times, took out his pocket-handkerchief, and began to wipe his glasses. Mrs. Bird, seeing the defenceless condition of the enemy's territory, had no more conscience than to push her advantage.

"I should like to see you doing that, John—I really should! Turning a woman out of doors in a snowstorm, for instance; or may be you'd take her up and put her in jail, wouldn't you? You would make a great hand at that!"

"Of course, it would be a very painful duty," began Mr. Bird, in a moderate tone.

"Duty, John! don't use that word! You know it isn't a duty—it can't be a duty! If folks want to keep their slaves from running away, let 'em treat 'em well,—that's my doctrine. If I had slaves (as I hope I never shall have), I'd risk their wanting to run away from me, or you either, John. I tell you folks don't run away when they are happy; and when they do run, poor creatures! they suffer enough with cold and hunger and fear, without everybody's turning against them; and, law or no law, I never will, so help me God!"

"Mary! Mary! My dear, let me reason with you."

"I hate reasoning, John,—especially reasoning on such subjects. There's a way you political folks have of coming round and round a plain right thing; and you don't believe in it yourselves, when it comes to practice. I know *you* well enough, John. You don't believe it's right any more than I do; and you wouldn't do it any sooner than I."

Ironically, during their debate, a runaway slave named Eliza comes to the Bird's door shivering from her tough journey from Kentucky. John Bird completely changes his way once he sees her in distress:

"I wonder who and what she is!" said Mr. Bird at last, as he laid it down.

"When she wakes up and feels a little rested, we will see," said Mr. Bird.

"I say, wife! said Mr. Bird, after musing in silence over the newspaper."

"Well, dear!"

"She couldn't wear one of your gowns, could she, by letting down, or such matter? She seems to be rather larger than you are."

A quite perceptible smile glimmered on Mr. Bird's face, as she answered, "We'll see."

Another pause, and Mr. Bird broke out, "I say, wife!"

"Well! What now?"

"Why, there's that old bombazine cloak, that you keep on purpose to put over me when I take my afternoon's nap; you might as well give her that,—she needs clothes."

Just like that a senator from Ohio, who was preaching for an unjust law, goes against it. Where does that sort of empathy come from? Why does he cry the way he does below?

Our senator was a statesman, and of course could not be expected to cry, like other mortals; and so he turned his back to the company, and looked out the window, and seemed particularly busy in clearing his throat and wiping his spectacle glasses, occasionally blowing his nose in a manner that was calculated to excite suspicion, had anyone been in a state to observe critically.

*

29

From Mrs. Shelby crying for Tom and his family to Dill feeling dizzy about the injustice of the trial to the senator and to Lee bending down to reach for the bird, all have something in common: all followed the words of Christ in Matthew 7:12 when he said: "So in everything, do unto to others as they would have them do unto you, for this sums up the Law and Prophets." They also followed one of the most challenging pieces of scripture of all time when Jesus said in Matthew 25:41: "I tell you the truth, whatever you did for one of the least of my brothers of mine, you did for me."

Every person in each instance was "above" the other that was being cried for: Mrs. Shelby was a rich white aristocrat, while Chloe and her family were slaves who weren't considered anywhere close to whites. Dill, even though just a young boy, was far above any black person in the southern town of Maycomb, yet he was noticeably distraught by the injustice that they were receiving. Then there is the senator and statesman, who has the empathy to cry. Finally, who would have ever thought that the most decorated war general on either side would be so meek as to care for a little baby bird?

Shocking moments have an incredible impact on human beings. We are creatures of nature who, whether we like it or not, are used to a routine. In that case, when we are shocked, or out of a routine, we remember that moment due to its rarity. It's not for anyone to say whether we remember moments in our lives that shocked us for the better or the worse, but it would be unfathomable for Aunt Chloe, Raymond, and that sweet baby bird to forget all those tears poured out for them by others.

2

Loving Our Enemies

If there is any tenet or teaching in Christianity that seems coun-terintuitive, unintelligent, and irrational, it is the commandment to love our enemies. Our society is oftentimes a meritocracy, or, in short, you get what you deserve. This means that in everyday inter-actions with others we treat people how they treat us. It only makes sense; why would you help someone who has hurt you? If anything, we follow the mantra of "you deserve what you get," so we should treat them just as poorly.

The problem with this way of thinking is that it lacks all hope and it is somewhat hypocritical of us to do this to another human being. We could have all been called enemies of God, but instead we are called friends of his through His Son. Because we are made in God's image and can have the potential to become more Christ-like every day, we need to play the role of Christ and see that speck of light in one another, even if it does not seem visible. It only makes sense considering that Christ did the same for us.

It is our natural instinct to look our sin dead in the eye and deny that we have any. For instance, if someone were to ask another if he had any enemies, he would most likely respond with a chuckle and say, "Of course not." However, if we delve further into our life and look at everyday occurrences through a closer lens, we will find that we do face enemies every day; we just might not call them as such. For example, if a taxi driver cuts off soccer-mom in heavy Atlanta traffic, her natural impulse might be to retaliate against the driver.

Often times, it can be harder on the person who commits a bad deed than on the person who had it done to them. The doer of the bad deed can quickly become the debtor. Looking at the reasons for this is an important thing to consider. This is one of the most unselfish maneuvers that the persecuted can do because it is making your own self vulnerable when that person should actually have all the power. In order to do this, the person cannot be living for themselves. In fact, they cannot even be living for the approval of others around them. This person has to be living for a different purpose.

A fine example of this is illustrated in *To Kill a Mockingbird* when Atticus responds to an enemy who has clearly done a wrong toward him. After the case, even though Bob Ewell won, he is angry at Atticus for making him out to be a liar. Ewell tracks him down and does one of the most despicable actions a human can do to another human: he spit on him.

If an outsider of Maycomb was looking at the specific set of circumstances, he would think that it would have been the other way around. If anyone had the right to spit on a person, it was Atticus. He was the one who had just lost a court case in which the verdict was clearly unjust. He was the one who took the case that nobody would ever want in the first place. Ironically, he, and not Ewell was the grown man who had the decency and kindness to treat Mayella with the respect that she so desperately needed but never got from her father. Yet, he was the one who had to pull out his handkerchief to wipe the spit off his face.

Apparently, all of the town would have agreed with the above observations of the situation. One neighbor told Atticus's children to go to their backyard, but more importantly he uttered the phrase that epitomizes gossip: "Ain't you heard yet? It's all over town."

With this commotion, it's easy to understand why everyone was so interested: they wanted to see how Atticus would respond to the evil man. However, Atticus didn't seem too interested in playing the role of a teenage drama queen. All he said about the situation was "I wish Bob Ewell wouldn't chew tobacco." For most of us, this seems preposterous for Atticus to say this. If there was ever a time to fight and say something about someone who hurt you, it would have been then. For human beings, there is no word we like more than when we have any sort of wrong or pain done to us: that word is justice and it is always referring to *our* justice. When we inflict any sort of pain on another, oftentimes we will call that in itself justice. In other words, we like to keep justice to ourselves.

So why did Atticus say this after he has been treated with such maliciousness by Ewell? This is because Atticus still seemed to think that he had an *advantage* over Ewell. He knew that he was possibly the most respected man in town and knew that his actions would have serious consequences, either negative or positive throughout the town. All of this leads to an interesting point, one that is rarely brought up in conversation for fear that we might offend someone. Unfortunately, that fear is actually driven by pure pride.

When people speak of having an advantage over someone, they often feel as if they have to tread on sharp glass. There is no need to do this because none of us created our own advantages. They were given to us by God. However, we do need to tread lightly on how we use our own advantages to help others. In what has come to be known as Robert E. Lee's "Definition of a Gentleman," he illustrates how we display our advantages over others:

> The forbearing use of power does not only form a touchstone, but the manner in which an individual enjoys certain advantages over the others is a test of a true gentleman.

> The power which the strong have over the weak, the employer over the employed, the educated over the unlettered, the experienced over the confiding, even the clever over the silly; the forbearing or inoffensive use of all this power or authority, or a total abstinence from it when the case admits it, will show the gentleman in a plain light.

> The gentleman does not needlessly and unnecessarily remind an offender of a wrong he may have committed against him. He cannot only forgive, he can forget; and he strives for that nobleness of self and mildness of character which impart sufficient strength to let the past be but the past. A true man of honor feels humbled when he cannot help humbling others.

Many times, we are afraid to admit we have certain advantages over others because it makes us feel as if we have a certain responsibility. Atticus does not fear this however. Even if Atticus were to admit his advantage, or know about it, what sets him apart is the manner in which he displays that certain advantage. Another reason for the significance of Atticus's action draws from the position and reputation he has in town. He was educated, came from a good family, and was friendly. Many people in the town look to his actions and follow them whatever they might be. Usually, when we our-selves are in a position or power, we like to look to see how we can use it to control others instead of realizing that we need to control ourselves that much more because of the position we are now in.

We must understand that everyone isn't quite like Atticus, how-ever. His own children certainly aren't. His daughter has another way of dealing with Bob Ewell, after all Miss Maudie said that "At-ticus was the deadest shot in Maycomb County in his time." Scout is of course referring to the fact that Atticus could easily shoot Ewell at the drop of a hat if he wants to. Much to Scout's dismay however Jem reminds his sister that Atticus had formerly told them that "havin' a gun around's an invitation for somebody to shoot you." Although these simple words might not be heralded in the land of religious academia, they ring true as any and can change our rela-tionships right here and now.

So many times, when we feel hurt by others, the first person we rush to see if he is doing alright is our self. It makes sense; if we are the one who has the broken wound, all energy feelings, emotion, and time should be directed toward our own healing.

However, that is not what the Rev. Martin Luther King Jr. has taught us to do. King once said that "life's most persistent and ur-gent question is 'what are you doing for others?'" It is so easy to get caught up in what we must do to please ourselves. However great capitalism is, it does not work effectively, if at all, without consump-tion. The more consumption there is, the better our economy is, but a great economy does not always produce happy people. How many times have you heard someone who came from wealth in America go into a third-world country and come back saying that although the people had nothing, they were much happier than the people in the United States?

If a bully were to push an innocent kid down on the playground, it makes sense to care for the innocent kid, but if the kid is still innocent, in the long run he will be just fine. The bully is the one we need to be the most worried about because we want him to break free of his destructive ways. Atticus certainly feels this way about Ewell. He may have been inspired to do this by the actions of Christ in the events leading up to the crucifixion. If we were the most important person in the world and were being crucified, we would naturally be calling for a foul. Christ even in that moment, wasn't calling for the foul, he *defended* them saying in Luke 23.34: "Father, forgive them, for they do not know what they are doing."

Atticus's response to Ewell is eerily similar to Christ's response at his own crucifixion. Of course, it all starts with standing in another person's shoes, the most difficult thing to do as a human being.

See if you stand in Bob Ewell's shoes a minute. I destroyed his last shred of credibility at that trial, if he had any to begin with. The man had to have some kind of comeback, his kind always does. So if spitting in my face and threatening me saved Mayella Ewell one extra beating, that's something I'll gladly take. He had to take it out on somebody and I'd rather it would be me than that household of children out there. You understand?

*

Many times, in order for businesses and governments to best hold themselves accountable, they must take a hard look at their mission statements or constitution. A hard look involves making sure the organization is *doing* what it says in the writing; *dreaming* about it does not count. The best way to get a hard look is not to look at sentences but at specific phrases where the words convey what the organization is all about. For example:

Stand in shoes—It's obvious that we are going to stand in shoes. What's not so obvious is *whose* shoes they are going to be. Atticus chooses unselfishly to stand in Ewell's.

A minute—A lot can be said in a minute. Misguided e-mails or texts can be typed and sent in a minute. A lie can be said in a minute, a murder's sentencing can be said in a minute.

I destroyed—If the townspeople were to see these words, the last person who they would pin them on would be Atticus Finch. He hasn't been a destroyer but rather a builder for the town. The *first* person who they would pin them on instead is Bob Ewell. He has destroyed many aspects of his life including his family, his daughter's life and self-esteem, and other people and things. It is safe to say however at this particular juncture that he hasn't been able to destroy the person he wished to destroy the most: Atticus Finch.

Most of the time it is not the secure hearted who enjoy hurting others but the insecure-hearted. You might not have ever heard these two terms, but there is a reason for linking them. A man's heart is only strong when it is safe, and it is only safe when it is secured in something strong. A man who is worth $10 million can be more secure than a man who has $10,000 to his name. If a man is secure in money, $100 million might not even be enough. John Steinbeck said it best in *The Pearl* when he said: "For it is said that humans are never satisfied, that you give them one thing and they want something more." If a person finds security in any other than what Atticus find security in, he is going to make Bob Ewell type decisions, "his kind always does."

Spitting in my face—The difference between the common phrase and how it is being used here is that it is being used literally. This phrase is synonymous with some of the worst descriptions such as "being stabbed in the back, hung out to dry"—things we wouldn't wish upon another person, certainly not ourselves. However, Atticus *does* wish this upon himself. We see why he does this in the next phrase we critique.

Saved—It doesn't take long to tie Atticus's response to Christ's response at accepting death on the cross to die for our sins. Both acts live out the Golden Rule in a profound way. It is fitting that the Golden Rule is called just that. Gold is valuable, but it is hard to find in us because of our natural disposition to be selfish. Saving is special because it means that the person who is to be saved must be in a vulnerable position, which is never easy.

Extra—Oftentimes, as humans we feel like the word "extra" doesn't mean too much. An economist might agree with this statement as well due to a phenomenon in economics known as "diminishing marginal utility." For instance, if you were to go to a doughnut shop and order 12 doughnuts and get an extra one, the consumer would appreciate the gesture but not think too much about it. At the same time, the word "extra" can mean a tremendous amount. For instance, if someone gets something worthwhile that is very valuable, he is very content. No one is ever going to complain if he buys a $500 phone and gets one free. However, when the tables are turned and the extra becomes something negative, people will do whatever it takes to avoid it, whether it is one extra report at the office, one extra chore for a child, or anything else like that. However, this extra choice ends up benefitting us in some way. The extra report compiled by the employee might get him in good with his boss or get him a raise one day. The chore done by the kid might well avoid having his mom nag him that day. But why would anybody in the world want to take on an extra task *himself*, one that would be a negative one that provided no incentive for us doing so? This type of person does exist in the world, the most prominent example being Jesus Christ, who took on an "extra" death for us and prayed to God that his will not be done, but God's. There is no doubt that Atticus was more than happy to take a beating for Mayella, just like Christ would die on the cross for us.

Gladly—Atticus says that he would gladly take an extra beating. There is a big difference between just taking a beating for somebody and gladly taking it. I have heard many times of people being quality acts or "intentional." I suppose this is a decent goal to shoot for, but there is a higher goal that is much more "sustainable" and "consistent." It is certainly not easy, as Uncle Tom remained with Cassy when they were speaking of Christ's generosity and courage. "If we could only keep that 'ar! It seemed so natural to him, and we have to fight so hard for it! O Lord, help us! O blessed Lord Jesus, do help us."

Rather than being intentional, which means we have to try with all our might the rest of our lives, why don't we train ourselves so these acts become natural? It certainly would make our lives easier. I'm sure you can think of some people in your life that will do something generous for you but will want something back in return for them, which makes their graciousness a bit awkward for you. It's similar to someone who says call me anytime, but doesn't truly mean it, and calling up another person who said call me up anytime and did mean it.

Out There— We have all met the types of people in our lives that are either "out there" or the people who live "out there." Neither is meant as a compliment. In fact, the narrator comments that "Atticus said the Ewells had been the disgrace of Maycomb for three generations. None of them had done an honest day's work in his recollection … They were people, but they lived like animals."

They certainly sound like people who were "out there" and lived "out there" even according to Atticus. The strange thing is that made Atticus more eager to help them. It is painful to write this because it is humbling, demoralizing, and self-defeating, but the fact of the matter is that we are all just like the Ewells in that from our sin we are all "out there." Luckily, just like the Ewells, we have Somebody to save us.

*

Because Tom was just a slave, Tom was consistently treated as being both "out there" and from "out there." The person who treated him like that the most was his final slave master, Simon Legree.

Christ didn't understand things such as market research, positioning, the Gallup poll, and the "I scratch your back if you scratch mine" philosophy. Luckily, Christ doesn't say to us to stay "out there," but he tells us to come over here and have our backs scratched even if all we have done is stabbed him in the back. If Christ of all people treats others as if there is nobody "out there," we should learn to do the same.

In chapter 1, I discuss how Tom dealt with being sold into slavery. Later in the book, he is dealt with another tough trial. This time, he has to deal with someone who stands for the opposite of everything for which he stands. This can be the toughest thing in dealing with enemies. Even if we are in the right, so to speak, it is impossible to force our views upon other people, even if it would ultimately help them. This is the passage in which the colloquial phrase "Uncle Tom" originated from. Further analysis of the text, however, reveals that this phrase is used with false premises. Tom does submit to his authorities … sometimes.

Much of the time, in our analysis of our lives and in the Bible in particular, we see things in black and white. While this is important in some cases, it is not a good mentality in all circumstances. Micah 6:8b, one of the most challenging biblical verses, describes two important qualities working in unison with each other: "To act justly and to love mercy and to walk humbly with your God."

When Legree is weighing the cotton that the each of the slaves has picked, "slowly the weary, dispirited creatures wound their way into the room, and, with crouching reluctance, presented their baskets to be weighed." The slaves were weary and dispirited not only from picking cotton all day but also because of their anxiety over whether they had picked enough cotton to satisfy their master. Tom tries to help a lady by giving her some of his own cotton. Unfortunately, even with the extra cotton, she doesn't make the necessary weight, leaving her the recipient of these harsh words by Legree: "What, you lazy beast! Short again! Stand aside, you'll catch it, pretty soon."

Quickly after Legree orders the flogging, the slaves realize that this would be no ordinary flogging: Tom would be the one who was to whip the woman. However, the plan wasn't going to work because Tom was going to refuse to do the flogging. Even after Tom receives repeated blows from Legree, he still denies Legree three times. It is often easy to worry about what type of *experience* we are having in our faith instead of looking at it as a *reality*. This is the most dangerous path a believer can go down because being a Christian and serving Christ is not about the experience, but the mundane and difficult day-to-day tasks that the Bible teaches us. Legree tries to reason with Tom by telling him that he bought Tom and that he should obey him because he is the master. Tom, however, is in no way afraid of Legree: "No! No! No! My soul ain't yours, Mas'r! You haven't bought it, ye can't buy it! It's been bought for and paid for, by one that is able to keep it; no matter, no matter, you can't harm me!"

Tom shows here that he is not going to be walked over and at the same times hurts his enemy with his piercing walk toward Christ. Many times, our enemies like to draw us in and make it seem like that is the only way to avoid being harmed. If we can learn the difference between acting out our faith as a reality, versus an experience, we don't have to be caught off guard in this way. The most confusing aspect of dealing with our enemies is that we often have a misguided view of what being walked over is all about. "Tom stood perfectly submissive; and yet Legree could not hide from himself that his power over his bond thrall was somehow gone."

3

Are You Willing to Bend Down?

We live in a harsh world, much of which is driven by consumerism or competition from other people's insecurities. Our water isn't clean enough, so we end up buying bottled water. The media, our own friends, and even our own family tell us sometimes that we aren't enough so why shouldn't we feel a natural sense of rejection and inadequacy?

> It was the first word of kindness the child ever heard in her life; and the sweet tone and manner struck strangely on the wild, rude heart, and a sparkle of something like a tear shone in the keen, round, glittering eye; but it was followed by the short laugh and habitual grin. No! the ear had that had never heard anything but abuse is strangely incredulous of anything so heavenly as kindness, and Topsy only thought Eva's speech something funny and inexplicable,—she did not believe it.

In *Uncle Tom's Cabin,* Topsy, a young slave, causes a lot of trouble on the plantation. It turns out that she had a rough past and can't trust anyone. While some of us may not have gone through the troubles that Topsy has gone through, many of us can attest to the fact that we often don't believe someone when they tell us that they are truly there for us. Encouragement, if nothing else, gives us a license to live in a place in which we were originally created and a place where we can be one day with the help of Jesus Christ. There is no doubt that God is omnipotent and his power is all-surpassing, but how are we supposed to know that if we have never visually seen God for ourselves? It is a pretty good question and one that many people have about Christianity.

In a quote that is often attributed to Ghandi, Bara Gada once said, "Jesus is ideal and wonderful, but you *Christians*—you are not like him." Gada has a valid point, at least to an extent. As Christians, we can't earn our way to heaven so it is certainly likely that a Jew, Muslim, Hindu, or agnostic could be more moral than us. However, Gada has a pretty good point because studies show that people are influenced by people they like and are willing to follow whatever they believe in. Gada wanted to see Christ in other people and, apparently, he couldn't. Gada is not the only one who thought this way: St. Clair in *Uncle Tom's Cabin* also goes on to say:

> Religion! Is what you hear at church religion? Is that which can bend and turn, and descend and ascend, to fit every crooked phase of selfish, worldly society, religion? Is that religion which is less scrupulous, less generous, less just, less considerate for man, than even my own ungodly, worldly, blinded nature? No! When I look for religion, I must look for something above me, and not something beneath.

*

No matter what denomination a Christian is, I think most can agree that no one has ever seen God face to face. This is the exact reason as Christians why we need to become agents of Christ and spread his unselfish nature to all mankind. The only way to see God on Earth is to see God through other people. How is a server at a fast food restaurant supposed to see God in you if you don't even look him in the eye when you order? Telling people about Christ has an impact on people in one way, but being Christlike toward others can have a far greater return on investment. It is true as Christians we technically have no duty. We all have unmerited grace, and if we accept Christ into our heart, we will go to heaven. With that said, however, Christ also says that "if you love me, you will obey me." Part of obeying is to love our fellow neighbor.

Although I am glad to live in a capitalist society, it is interesting to think about how different life would be if we lived how some of the earliest Christians lived. Acts 2:44 states that "all the believers were together and had everything in common." While this sounds like Communism, it actually is different from what many people think of as modern Communism because people were not forced to do this; they did so in spontaneity. When I was in Greek life in college at Samford University in Birmingham, Alabama, my girlfriend's sorority made each member pay money to a certain charity. This didn't seem like charity at all and when my fraternity attempted to do something similar, I was offended. No one likes charity of goodness that is forced because people quickly realize whether that charity is genuine or not. Forced charity does not come from up above but down below. The reason for this is because it is temporal and not eternal.

Many people use the phrase that "life is too short to do this or that:" I take the opposite approach. I think that life is too long not to have a job that you like or to not be around people you enjoy. Life is too long to have a rocky relationship with your spouse, and life is too long to go through the down points just by yourself. That is why Jesus constantly charges us to look after one another. Suicide is one of the saddest circumstances that can occur because it is something that can usually be prevented. God is not just going to send some ray of light to help that person from committing suicide. That is where we must help each other.

*

In the town of Maycomb in *To Kill a Mockingbird*, there is a group of white women known as the Missionary Society Ladies, who have tea and crumpets in each other's home and talk about how they can help save the African people. Lee's point in the book is to point out the sheer hypocrisy that the ladies portray daily. Here, they are supposedly worrying about the status of Africans in a faraway place while they discriminate against the black people in their own town. Scout is forced to sit in these meetings and hates doing so because she is a tomboy and not a Maycomb lady. More often than not, the reason we succumb to depression is because we do not feel like we fit into a crowd. People not only hate to be alone, they hate being criticized for the actions they have taken alone. Miss Maudie makes sure that Scout doesn't feel alone when Miss Stephanie tells Scout: "Well, you won't get very far until you start wearing dresses more often." Luckily, Scout ended up being okay: "Miss Maudie's hand closed tightly on mine, and I said nothing. Its warmth was enough."

Since none of us will see God on Earth, we face an uphill battle to show others that God truly exists. The only way to measure if we are doing enough is to look through the perspective of the other person. This is much easier said than done because, as humans, we respond to incentives and, unfortunately, these incentives typically involve making ourselves happy. In dealings with other people, the person who says I can never do enough versus enough already is a friend I would like to have. Miss Maudie was that person for Scout.

As I have stated earlier, it is natural for people to respond to incentives. Put an attractive girl in a bar and eventually a man will try to go talk to her. Increase a sales person's bonus structure and she will work longer hours and make more sales calls. All of these are logical, so it makes perfect sense to ask why would someone go out of his way to do something kind for someone else? It is understandable that one might live out The Golden Rule for someone in his family or someone in his own group of people. But why would someone go out of his way to do something kind for someone who cannot give him anything in the future? There is no scientific explanation for altruism. It is interesting to see what level of altruism different people display. It is certainly impressive that Bill Gates will give $10 million dollars away, but isn't it more impressive for a struggling fast-food worker to give a few dollars in an offering plate?

One example of Robert E. Lee showing his Christian duty was at a church service in Richmond. A black man, who no one had ever seen before, came to church that day and took part in communion. Before communion was even given, he went up to the communion rail by himself and got down on his knees. People were quite surprised that he would do this. However, that did not stop Lee from joining the black man and kneeling beside him. People went on to follow Lee and went up to the rail with him. Lee was certainly not forced to do this act, but he did so because he knew it was the right action to take.

One of the most profound quotes that Lee ever said was, "There is no more dangerous experiment than that of undertaking to be one thing before a man's face and another behind his back." Why do we talk behind peoples back? Is it because we truly care about them? Absolutely not. We do so in order to lift ourselves up, make us feel better about ourselves. If we really cared about what someone was doing, we would tell them directly to their face because we know that is the best way to take on a problem. Have you ever heard someone talk behind your back? It makes you feel helpless and you are sad to know that person has this particular view of you.

Talking behind someone's back is a very passive aggressive action to take, and it leaves the person to whom it is being done completely defenseless. The saddest person in this type of gossip is not victim but the one doing the talking because it shows how weak and insecure that person actually is. Talking about others is also counterproductive because instead of actually making the problem any better, it makes the problem worse. While the gossiper believes that the problem is getting solved, nothing is actually happening.

In her concluding remarks, in *Uncle Tom's Cabin*, Harriet Beecher Stowe remarks:

An atmosphere of sympathetic influence encircles every human being; and the man or woman who *feels* strongly, healthily and justly, on the great interests of humanity, is a constant benefactor to the human race. See, then, to your sympathies in this matter! Are they in harmony with the sympathies of Christ? or are they swayed and perverted by the sophistries of worldly policy?

A hard aspect of living the Golden Rule is that we must get out of ourselves, and to do so means that we must get *out of this world.* What does the world *strongly* mean in this instance?

Strongly—What makes someone strong? Is it their temperament? Is it their appearance? Or is it how they treat others? For me, my favorite story to tell about true strength occurred in my father's law office when I was in high school. The office celebrates everyone's birthday by having the birthday person select their own cake and all of the staff goes into the conference room to celebrate. It was my father's birthday and everyone gathered around the table to celebrate as the founding partner and one of the top three lawyers in the state was ready to make some remarks. Even though the day was about him, to him the day is never about just him. He started off by saying how fortunate they were to have Willene, the cleaning lady, there celebrating as well. He explained that she had been at the office for nine years and provided great value to the firm. I can still remember the looks on people's faces; people didn't even know what to say. Many times, in our lives it is tough to remember that we are not the center of the universe, but rather one tiny aspect of it. With that said, however, one tiny little speck in the universe can do wonders for shaping humanity.

*

One of the most misunderstood characters in the Bible is Pontius Pilate. He could have been the hero of the whole entire Bible had it not be for one thing: the mob. I've realized over time that the most dangerous opposition to morality is a mob. People change when they are in a group, and it is rarely for the better. Although Pilate gets a lot of hate for being the one to send Jesus Christ to the cross, it is the crowd that he had to deal with that should shoulder much of the blame. In *To Kill a Mockingbird*, there is a crowd of people at the jail who want to get in to kill Tom Robinson. Dill, Jem, and Scout look out from afar and wait in the square until Scout senses trouble. Eventually, they all run up to the jail to make sure Atticus is okay. Scout is the one who stops the crowd, but not because she has a gun. Later, Atticus and Jem have a conversation about it all.

"Mr. Cunningham's basically a good man," he said. "He just has his blind spots along with the rest of us."

Jem spoke. "Don't call that a blind spot. He'd a' killed you last night when he first went there."

"He might have hurt me a little," Atticus conceded, "but son, you'll understand folks a little better when you're older. A mob's always made up of people, no matter what. Mr. Cunningham was part of a mob last night, but he was still a man. Every mob in every little Southern town is always made up of people, you know— doesn't say much for them, does it?"

"I'll say not," said Jem.

"So it took an eight-year-old child to bring 'em to their senses, didn't it?" said Atticus. "That proves something—that a gang of wild animals can be stopped, simply because they're still human. Hmph, maybe we need a police force of children … You children last night made Walter Cunningham stand in my shoes for a minute. That was enough."

I've found in my own life, the most evil things seem to occur in a mob. A great example of this would occur annually in my fraternity at Samford University. Older members of the fraternity would woo pledges to steal Christmas decorations from outlining towns in Birmingham. While I never stole any Christmas decorations myself or encouraged our pledges to do, I still did not have the guts to tell the members of the fraternity to stop the theft. There was only one thing that I was afraid of: my light. According to Marriane Williamson, author of *Return to Love*:

> Our deepest fear is not that we are inadequate. Our deepest fear is that we are powerful beyond measure. It is our light, not our darkness that most frightens us. We ask ourselves, Who am I to be brilliant, gorgeous, talented, and fabulous? Actually, who are you not to be? You are a child of God. Your playing small does not serve the world. There is nothing enlightened about shrinking so that other people will not feel insecure around you. We are all meant to shine, as children do. We were born to make manifest the glory of God that is within us. It is not just in some of us; it is in everyone and as we let our own light shine, we unconsciously give others permission to do the same. As we are liberated from our own fear, our presence automatically liberates others.

Too often, we shrink when we around others just so we will not make them feel inferior. This is an absolute insult to God when we do this. He made us to make manifest the glory of God that is within us. In the heat of the moment however it is much easier to be comfortable than to stand up for what is right.

4

Understanding and Passing Down

Oftentimes, it is tough to live the Golden Rule because we never get to know the other person. In *To Kill a Mockingbird*, Judge Taylor says that "people generally see what they look for, and hear what they listen for." This doesn't seem like too complex of a situation after all. Even when we dispense advice we will often draw conclusions that seem more fitting to us than the other person.

One of the main premises of *To Kill a Mockingbird* involves the three children, Dill, Scout, and Jem, exploring and discovering who Boo Radley really is. They do this by spying on him, playing games based on him with one another, and in general thinking up spooky scenarios involving him. They make him out to be an outcast, a villain, and someone who people would not want to be around. This should sound familiar if you know the New Testament because this is exactly how Jesus was portrayed as well in some circles. Boo Radley is the saving figure in the book just as Christ is the saving figure of the New Testament. He ends up saving Jem from Bob Ewell who was trying to avenge what Atticus did to him in the courtroom. When Scout realizes what Boo did for Jem, her attitude completely changes. While he was once an outcast to her, he now becomes part of the family.

One reason that we never get to know other people is because it requires us to become vulnerable to other people. To become vulnerable not only requires work but also requires courage. Many people are unwilling to admit their blind spots or flaws. However, when this happens, a whole new world is opened up because it enables both parties to be real with each other. One of my favorite people is one of my best friends named Carson Pyles. The reason I respect him so much is that he is the most secure person I have ever met in my life. I do not know where he gets that security, but it is like a breath of fresh air. I find myself having to constantly "sell" myself to get approval, but I never have to do that with him. He likes me just the way I am.

Without loving oneself first, it is impossible to love others. Many people think that arrogant people are in fact that way because they hold a lofty view of themselves. This is not true, however. Arrogant people are that way because of the deep insecurity rooted within them. Do we ever really give a chance for people to be comfortable with themselves? The simple answer is no. As human beings, we try to act religious and generous at funerals *after* someone has died. Do you realize how much it would mean to the person if you told them before they passed away?

*

To get to know someone requires a lot of work. It requires patience, effort, and most of all, looking at life through another person's perspective other than your own. There are many characters throughout *To Kill a Mockingbird* who accomplish this feat: Atticus, Calpurnia, Boo Radley, Miss Maudie, and others. The people that lack that ability are Scout (at times), Bob Ewell, and the mob at the jail and to name a few. Entering a relationship, whether it is a romantic one or just a friendship, takes a knack that some of us can never grasp. Boo Radley seems to understand it from the beginning however. At one point in the novel, the children dare each other to go up to Boo Radley's door. They run away when they sense danger and Jem gets caught up in the fence. Later, Jem tells Scout:

"When I went back for my breeches—they were all in a tangle when I was gettin' out of 'em. I couldn't get 'em loose. When I went back—" Jem takes a deep breath. "When I went back, they were folded across the fence . . . like they were expectin' me."

"Across—"

"And something else—" Jem's voice was flat. "Show you when we get home. They'd been sewed up. Not like a lady sewed 'em, like somethin' I'd try to do. All crooked. It's almost like—"

"—somebody knew you were coming back for 'em."

Jem shuddered. "Like somebody was readin' my mind . . . like somebody could tell what I was gonna do. Can't anybody tell what I'm gonna do lest they know me, can they Scout?"

Jem's question was an appeal. I reassured him: "Can't anybody tell what you're gonna do lest they live in the house with you, and even I can't tell sometimes."

As mentioned earlier, Radley, along with Atticus, is seen in a Christlike way. He seems to be omnipotent later in the book when he saves the lives of both Scout and Jem. It is interesting when Jem makes the comment to Scout, "Can't anybody tell what I'm going to do lest they know me, can they Scout?"

Scout responds with, "Can't anybody tell what you're gonna do lest they live in the house with you, and even I can't tell sometimes."

To live life to the pinnacle, we must realize that God knows us and knows us very well. We also must trust that he knows what is best for us, even though it doesn't seem like a great outcome at the time. I am glad that I was denied some of the jobs for which I applied. I am glad that things didn't work out with every girl I dated. I never thought growing up that I would be on multiple medications in my twenties. But I know that God made me this way for a reason because he has a plan for me and every other human being. The ultimate assurance on the Golden Rule to us from God is Jeremiah 29:11 when it says, "For I know the plans I have for you," declares the Lord, "plans to prosper you and not to harm you, plans to give you a hope and a future." We can take comfort in that fact that just as Boo Radley watches out for the kids that one night, God watches over us as he lives out the Golden Rule in our lives.

Teaching the Golden Rule to Our Children

Ultimately, however, even as you read this book, the likelihood of it having an impact on your future actions might be unlikely. According to a *First Rate Madness* by Nassir Ghaemi, "our basic temperaments are set by the time we reach kindergarten; studies show that those basic temperaments measured at age three persist and predict adult personality at age eighteen. From then onward as well, despite what many intuitively believe, our basic personality traits change little throughout adulthood and into old age. We may get wiser as we get older, but we do both become less introverted, or more open to experience, or less neurotic (to mention three personality traits.)"

Children pick up literally *everything* a parent does, whether it is drinking too much, how a husband treats his wife, even how a parent normally treats a janitor or fast food worker. For instance, if a father treats the concierge person at his work as an inferior person when he and his children go to his office building, there is a very high chance that the children will do the exact same thing. However, if the children notice that the parent actually engages that person in conversation, the children will follow their behavior. Even if children are bright, they often only understand aspects of life that are associated with certain things. If the parent acts kindly to only their friends at the country club, there are subliminal signals that the child receives: be nice to this group of people like their mother or father do. However, if five minutes later their mother or father doesn't show the same warmth and expressiveness to a waiter or waitress, it signals to the child that it is in fact "normal" and "okay" to treat the waiter or waitress like this.

Children are influenced by parents, but they are also influenced by other adults such as Sunday School teachers, coaches, teachers, and others. In my life, a mentor outside of my family was a golf coach at North Fulton Golf Course named Matt Adams. In a predominately white neighborhood, he stood out because he is African-American. My view of African-Americans was much different from most kids I grew up with because of my close friendship with Matt.

In *To Kill a Mockingbird*, Atticus Finch says that "the one thing that doesn't abide by majority rule is a person's conscience." While this seems to be true, we have to ask ourselves how we create a conscience in a person to begin with. Sure, we are naturally selfish as human beings, but can we be taught how to live out the Golden Rule or is it some innate disposition that we are born with? The power parents have over their child's ability to live out the Golden Rule should never be underestimated. For instance, my mother required us to write thank you notes as children. We were taught to say thank you to both our parents for every single meal we ate out, and when I had a meal with another family's parents, I would thank them as well. Even recently, an old family friend, Lindsay McGhee Kaufman gave a gift in my honor to a mental illness foundation because she could not attend an event I had invited her to. Many people claimed they would give a donation in my honor, but she actually did so, which was very special of her. She never even announced that she would do so, which made it even better.

My mother always encouraged me to write thank you notes. I played in a league called the Atlanta Junior Golf Association where we would play junior golf tournaments in the Atlanta area during the summer. Atlanta is hot and humid in the summer, and after one particular outing, the heat and poor play left me downtrodden. Others expressed dissatisfaction about the new golf course. As usual, my mother forced me to write a thank you note to the golf professional at the course. I explained to him that I had a pretty rough time on the course and that I did not score well, but that I appreciated the opportunity to play on his course. How did he respond to my letter? He himself wrote a thank you note back to me! Here is what the note said:

Thomas,

Thank you for taking the time to write a thank you note. Of the 81 players only 3 took the extra time to say thank you. I am sure you have wonderful parents! No matter how well you played, you have shown me that you are a gentleman—that is much more important than golf scores. Come back and visit!

5

Don't Be Normal

One reason why so many people struggle with living out the Golden Rule is because in order to live out the Golden Rule, you have to break social norms, which is difficult for people to do. We don't like to take chances doing so because we live in a culture obsessed with what other people think. Everyone can agree though that anything worthwhile, anything worth striving for, has some element of rarity to it.

One of the most fulfilling moments of my life came in 2016 when I served as the Sales Team Coach for Morehouse College. I got the position by literally walking in to the business building one day and asking the interim dean if I could help out with the sales program. I met with Dr. Cassandra Wells a few weeks later, and she was happy to have the help but wondered why on earth I would want to do it for free. The reason I wanted to do it was because I had a talent and would like to pass on that talent to others.

Those meetings with Dr. Wells, Professor Corrales, Armani Simmons, Justin Jones, James Jones, and Audtrell Williams were some of the most fulfilling hours I have ever spent on Earth. Seeing them improve their skills and sharpen their minds didn't just help them, it helped me. The highlight of our time together was when we went down to Orlando for a big competition. We ended up beating both UGA and Georgia Southern to become number one in the state.

Although I only made $.50 that whole year, it felt as if I was making seven-figures.

*

One of the most successful companies in the world is Apple. They have been ultra-successful because of the value the company's leadership places on disruptive innovation. Here is a quote at the beginning of one of Apple's summits:

> Here's to the crazy ones. The misfits. The rebels. The troublemakers. The round pegs in the square holes. The ones who see things differently. They're not fond of rules. And they have no respect for the status quo. You can quote them, disagree with them, glorify or vilify them. About the only thing you can't do is ignore them. Because they change things. They push the human race forward. And while some may see them as the crazy ones, we see genius. Because the people who are crazy enough to think they can change the world, are the ones who do. (Rob Siltanen)

We would not have Christianity today if Jesus respected the status quo. If Jesus's disciples had not risked their lives two thousand years ago, Christianity would not have multiplied from 12 disciples to 2 billion followers of Christ today.

In *Uncle Tom's Cabin*, when Tom goes out of his way to help the woman who had not picked as much cotton as he had, another woman disagrees with the act. She quips, "You know nothing about this place, or you wouldn't have done that. When you've been here a month, you'll be done helping anybody; you'll find it hard enough to take care of your own skin!" Tom's only response was, "The Lord forbid, Missis!"

This is what ultimate sacrifice is. A good parent will always agree to take on the pain that his or her on child has. This is in fact what Tom does. This portrays exactly what the Apple quote talks about doing. Was Tom a rebel to do what he did? Absolutely. Was he a bit crazy to what he did? For sure. He certainly saw things differently from most people as well. He saw serving others as more important than serving himself. He wasn't fond of rules and certainly didn't follow the status quo. He was glorified by some people and certainly hated by others. One thing is for sure though. You can't ignore these kinds of people because they push the human race forward. Tom was crazy to do what he did, but it is important to note that throughout history any Christian who has truly changed the religion has been deemed as crazy by others at some point.

*

I have refused to be normal in my actions to others because that is what Christ taught us. When I was a counselor at Camp Laney, there was a camper named Peyton Wolf who I had gotten to know through the years. Even though he was only 16 or 17 years old at the time, he knew he wanted to serve his country in the US Army. I respected this a great deal. I worked at the pool for three summers and Peyton didn't know how to swim. As a counselor, you had two free periods a day, and I usually spent these working out or reading a John Grisham book. However, Peyton needed to learn how to swim and I could teach him how to. Even though it was during my free time, I gave it up to teach Peyton how to swim. I can say it was the least I could do for someone who was willing to give up their life to serve me and my country. I've learned throughout life that you will never regret giving a part of yourself for someone else whether that be time or money.

*

In *Uncle Tom's Cabin*, Marie, who is Eva's mother, calls her strange on several occasions throughout the book. The first time is when one of the slaves is sick and she wants to help take care of her mom:

"Mamma, couldn't I take care of you one night—just one? I know I shouldn't make you nervous, and I shouldn't sleep. I often lie awake nights, thinking—"

"O, nonsense, child—nonsense!" said Marie; "you are such a strange child!"

"But may I, mamma? I think," she said, timidly, "that Mammy isn't well. She told me her head ached all the time, lately."

Later in the book, Marie warns Ophelia of what she thinks of Eva:

"And now," said Marie, "I believe I've told you everything; so that, when my next sick turn comes on, you'll be able to go forward entirely, without consulting me;—only about Eva,—she requires watching."

"She seems to be a good child, very," said Miss Ophelia; "I never saw a better child."

"Eva's peculiar," said her mother, "very. There are things about her so singular; she isn't like me, now, a particle;" and Marie sighed, as if this was a truly melancholy consideration.

Miss Ophelia in her own heart said, "I hope she isn't," but had prudence enough to keep it down.

"Eva always was disposed to be with servants; and I think that well enough with some children. Now, I always played with father's little negroes—it never did me any harm. But Eva somehow always seems to put herself on an equality with every creature that comes near her. It's a strange thing about the child. I never have been able to break her of it. St. Clare, I believe, encourages her in it. The fact is, St. Clare indulges every creature under this roof but his own wife."

Again Miss Ophelia sat in blank silence.

Later, St. Clare asks Eva which is better: having freedom for the slaves up North or having slavery as it is now in the South:

"I say, what do you think, Pussy?" said her father to Eva, who came in at this moment, with a flower in her hand.

"What about, papa?"

"Why, which do you like the best,—to live as they do at your uncle's, up in Vermont, or to have a house-full of servants, as we do?"

"O, of course, our way is the pleasantest," said Eva.

"Why so?" said St. Clare, stroking her head.

"Why, it makes so many more round you to love, you know," said Eva, looking up earnestly.

"Now, that's just like Eva," said Marie; "just one of her odd speeches."

"Is it an odd speech, papa?" said Eva, whisperingly, as she got upon his knee.

"Rather, as this world goes, Pussy," said St. Clare.

One of the most paradoxical aspects of people their seemingly incessant desire to seek approval from others. The paradox lies in the fact that the person who seeks approval does so in order to further himself. However, his fellow man is sinful, so the only direction he can go is backward.

As mentioned earlier, Luke 6:26 says, "Woe to you when all men speak well of you." People should really be seeking the approval of God in order to move forward. Mark Twain aptly said, "Whenever you find yourself on the side of the majority, it is time to reform (or pause and reflect)."

Getting hung up on what other human beings think is indefensible at best. Matthew 10:29–30 goes on: "Truly I tell you," Jesus replied, "no one who has left home or brothers or sisters or mother or father or children or fields for me and the gospel will fail to receive a hundred times as much in this present age: homes, brothers, sisters, mothers, children and fields—along with persecutions—and in the age to come eternal life." We are called by the Lord to think outside the box as humans, instead of thinking of our normal selfish desires. The first step in trying to live out the Golden Rule is to admit that as human beings we are naturally selfish. Until one believes this in their heart, they will never be able to change their ways and live a more fulfilling life.

If one were to ask a group of married couples who had been happily married for more than 25 years to describe one another, I think the last word they would use to describe the other spouse is normal. If the great leaders like Martin Luther King Jr. and Abraham Lincoln were normal, our country would not be the country it is today. Uncle Tom and Atticus are talked about so much to this day because they were not normal, they were abnormal. However, the word abnormal has a negative connotation to it even though it shouldn't.

As I mentioned earlier, shocking people for the right reasons is what we should all strive to do. To influence someone is not just to change their mind about something, but it is to change their point of view from a harsh point of view to a more empathetic one. We often wonder why others can't see our point of view. The reason for this is simple: we are programmed as humans to look after one thing: our own self-interest. There is nothing wrong with this per se, but it leaves someone to have a more unfulfilled life.

As much as we are hardwired as human beings to think about ourselves, there is something about us from above that enjoys helping others even if it is not our own family. Why do we as humans give so much to charity, why do we log in billions of hours of work volunteering? Is it because we have to find some meaning in our lives? In my own life, I have found that the best way to ease feelings of depression is to help others. There is something refreshing about giving a part of us to another person in need.

In Martin Luther King Jr.'s pivotal letter from the Birmingham Jail, he wrote that "oppressed people cannot remain forever. The yearning for freedom eventually manifests itself." King was speaking to the lack of civil rights in his day for African Americans, but what he says here really applies to all human beings living in America today. All of us want to be treated equally and all deserve to be treated this way regardless of whether someone is a CEO, a school teacher, or a short-order cook at a fast-food restaurant. If a CEO is really good, he/she wants to be treated as everyone else. A janitor likes to be recognized for his/her work as well. All of us have talents, which should not to be used for our own good but for the good of those around us. That is why God gave us talents in the first place.

In the letter from the Birmingham Jail, Martin Luther King went on further to say that

An unjust law is a human law that is not rooted in eternal law and natural law. Any law that uplifts human personality is just. Any law that degrades human personality is unjust. All segregation statutes are unjust because segregation distorts the soul and damages the personality. It gives the segregator a false sense of superiority and the segregated a false sense of inferiority.

Ultimately, segregation is wrong because it degrades human personality. Any time we judge someone based not on the content of their character, but rather based on something God-Given, it is wrong. From my own personal life, I have dealt with discrimination before firsthand. I had gone on a few dates with a beautiful young woman who lived in Birmingham, Alabama. We got along really well until I disclosed to her that I had a mental illness. After I explained to her that I had bipolar, she no longer wished to speak to me. To make matters worse she called herself a devout Christian and went to one of the more popular churches in Birmingham. Discrimination of any sort—whether discriminating against mental illness, against Jews in the Nazi regime, or against black Americans—doesn't live out the Golden Rule because it lacks empathy; it lacks the ability to see a point of view from the others perspective.

From an early age, parents (at least good parents) try to instill in their children a sense of fairness and equality. One of the first words we learn is *share*. While we might be sharing a toy or another cookie, what the parent is really coaching us to do is to *share* another person's perspective. It is impossible to share another person's perspective if we already have preconceived notions about them.

Even Abraham Lincoln did not think that black people should have civil rights during his presidency. The problem that Lincoln had as well as white southerners at the time was not that they were ignorant, but they never got into the shoes of the black people living in the United States at the time. They never took the time to realize that the black people couldn't read as well or speak as well as the whites because they did not have the proper training. The same racism that occurred back then unfortunately still occurs today in the black community.

*

There needs to be a sense of urgency when dealing with our fellow human beings. Waiting to do God's word is disobedience. Martin Luther King Jr. went on further to say in his letter from the Birmingham Jail:

> I had also hoped that the white moderate would reject the myth concerning time in relation to the struggle for freedom. I have just received a letter from a white brother in Texas. He writes:
>
> All Christians know that the colored people will receive equal rights eventually, but it is possible that you are in too great a religious hurry. It has taken Christianity almost two thousand years to accomplish what it has. The teachings of Christ take time to come to earth. Such an attitude stems from a tragic misconception of time, from the strangely irrational notion that there is something in the very flow of time that

will inevitably cure all ills. Actually, time itself is neutral; it can be used either destructively or constructively. More and more I feel that the people of ill will have used time much more effectively than have the people of good will. We will have to repent in this generation not merely for the hateful words and actions of the bad people but for the appalling silence of the good people. Human progress never rolls in on wheels of inevitability; it comes through the tireless efforts of men willing to be co-workers with God, and without this hard work, time itself becomes an ally of the forces of social stagnation. We must use time creatively, in the knowledge that the time is always ripe to do right. Now is the time to make real the promise of democracy and transform our pending national elegy into a creative psalm of brotherhood. Now is the time to lift our national policy from the quicksand of racial injustice to the solid rock of human dignity.

King makes very valid points in his statements here. He urged all white people to not delay in treating black people with the Golden Rule. Just as many southern leaders were late to denounce slavery 100 years back, there were southern leaders of that day as well that wanted to delay civil rights. King makes a very good point as well when he says that "time itself is neutral; it can be used either destructively or constructively." This is of course true in our places of work and school, but it is also true in how we treat each other as human beings. He makes an even better point when he says that "human progress never rolls in on wheels of inevitability; it comes through the tireless efforts of men willing to be co-workers with God, and without this hard work, time itself becomes an ally of the forces of social stagnation. We must use time creatively, in the knowledge that the time is always ripe to do right." For black people during the time of the civil rights movement, social stagnation hurt them the most. It continues to hurt us today as well.

*

In *To Kill a Mockingbird*, Tom Robinson admits that he feels sorry for Mayella Ewell. During this time, it was inconceivable for a black person to feel sorry for a white person because to feel sorry for a white person puts the black person at a higher status than the white person. Quickly, Tom realizes his mistake; it was the wrong thing to say because of social stagnation. Stagnation is a negative word. If a business or sports team is stagnant, it means that they aren't moving. Stagnation is the easy way out because of the safety it provides however.

6

An Extremist?

When judging another person, I never look for the big moments that test their character. I look for the small ones. Big moments carry a heroic aspect to them so there is a certain selfish incentive to make sure they are carried out to fruition. Small moments, however, never get any credit. This accentuates their value. The reason for this is because someone can see exactly what you are sacrificing, and that sacrifice lends itself to praise. Because of this, I believe that God made Jesus die on the cross not only for our sins, but he also had to wander for 40 days in the desert as shown here in Matthew 4:1-11:

Then Jesus was led by the Spirit into the wilderness to be tempted by the devil. After fasting forty days and forty nights, he was hungry. The tempter came to him and said, "If you are the Son of God, tell these stones to become bread." Jesus answered, "It is written: 'Man shall not live on bread alone, but on every word that comes from the mouth of God.' Then the devil took him to the holy city and had him stand on the highest point of the temple. "If you are the Son of God," he said, "throw yourself down. For it is written: 'He will command his angels concerning you, and they will lift you up in their hands, so that you will not strike your foot against a stone.'" Jesus answered him, "It is also written: 'Do not put the Lord your God to the test.'" Again, the devil took him to a very high mountain and showed him all the kingdoms of the world and their splendor. "All this I will give you," he said, "if you will bow down and worship me." Jesus said to him, "Away from me, Satan! For it is written: 'Worship the Lord your God, and serve him only.'" Then the devil left him, and angels came and attended him.

Just as Jesus made it through those challenging days, Tom is challenged by Legree:

"Have not many of us, in the weary way of life, felt, in some hours, how far easier it were to die than to live?

"The martyr, when faced even by a death of bodily anguish and horror, finds in the very terror of his doom a strong stimulant and tonic. There is a vivid excitement, a thrill and fervor, which may carry through any crisis of suffering that is the birth-hour of eternal glory and rest.

"But to live,—to wear on, day after day, of mean, bitter, low, harassing servitude, every nerve dampened and depressed, every power of feeling gradually smothered,—this long and wasting heart-martyrdom, this slow, daily bleeding away of the inward life, drop by drop, hour after hour,—this is the true searching test of what there may be in man or woman."

Stowe does a beautiful job of describing any mundane task of securing a stable healthy relationship: doing the small ordinary tasks of keeping a relationship is what keeps a relationship not only afloat but thriving. Sure, for a man to buy a $1,000 necklace on Valentine's Day for his spouse is certainly a nice gesture, but how much more impressive is it for that man to volunteer to go over vocabulary cards with his daughter who has a test the next day? There is a true vivid excitement when we know what we are doing is impressive and going to receive credit, but how much more impressive is it to do countless thankless tasks that receive no credit?

*

The word *extreme* is seen in our language as a negative word. We might say that speaker was "extreme," or it is extremely cold or hot outside if we notice tough weather. The great thinkers of our day such as Martin Luther King Jr. did not look at the word extreme as negative; he saw it as a positive word. Writing from the Birmingham Jail, King wrote:

> So the question is not whether we will be extremists, but what kind of extremists we will be. Will we be extremists for hate or for love? Will we be extremists for the preservation of injustice or for the extension of justice? In that dramatic scene on Calvary's hill three men were crucified. We must never forget that all three were crucified for the same crime—the crime of extremism. Two were extremists for immorality, and thus fell below their environment. The other, Jesus Christ, was an extremist for love, truth and goodness, and thereby rose above his environment. Perhaps the South, the nation and the world are in dire need of creative extremists.

Whether we admit it or not, we all are extremists. We might be extremists for making money and leading a comfortable life. We might be an extremist for acceptance and popularity. We might even be an extremist for pleasure. When I have been happiest in my own life, I have found the only way to achieve this goal is to be an extremist for others. Self-help books are not the answer to living a

71

fulfilling life. It's only when we realize that we need to put others first is when we find our true God-given value. We need to be extreme, we need to be bold, we need to go all out, but we need to do this all for others, not ourselves.

*

Atticus Finch is seen as extreme, and that is why he is the number one hero according to the American Film Institute. Much as I discussed earlier, there is an obsession in our culture of fitting in or being normal.

When speaking to Jem and Scout about the town of Maycomb, Miss Maudie remarks, "We're the safest folks in the world. We're so rarely called on to be Christians, but when we are, we've got men like Atticus to go for us." Pursuing safety in life is the subtlest sin in Christianity. We are warned throughout the Bible that to "eat, drink, and be merry" is distasteful to the Lord.

The reason we look up to figures such as Martin Luther King Jr. or Abraham Lincoln is because they were against the status quo. Going against the status quo can be daunting at times, but you have to go against it if you want to do anything meaningful in life. The reason for this is because life as we know it is in stagnation unless we take steps to change it. All of us have the power to bring heaven here on Earth; the only way to do that is to treat people the way you would like to be treated. It can be a challenge to love our enemies if we are ultimately seeking power over them: loving our enemies tells them that they can have power over us.

In *Uncle Tom's Cabin*, when Legree is about to kill Tom, it is amazing to look at how Tom treats him. Instead of being angry at him, Tom thinks in his head what Legree must do in order to save himself. He is willing to even sacrifice his own body to see his master saved. He says, "Mas'r, if you was sick, or in trouble, or dying, and I could save ye, I'd *give* ye my heart's blood; and if taking every drop of blood in this poor old body would save your precious soul, I'd give 'em freely, as the Lord gave his for me. O, Mas'r! don't bring this great sin on your soul! It will hurt you more than 'twill me! Do the worst you can, my troubles'll be over soon; but, if you don't repent, yours won't *never* end."

By Tom telling Legree that he would give his own blood to save Legree, he basically tells Legree that he already has all the power over Tom already. That is exactly what Jesus commands us to do when he says to love our enemies in Matthew 5:43–48: Here is the passage:

You have heard that it was said, "Love your neighbor and hate your enemy." But I tell you, love your enemies and pray for those who persecute you, that you may be children of your Father in heaven. He causes his sun to rise on the evil and the good, and sends rain on the righteous and the unrighteous. If you love those who love you, what reward will you get? Are not even the tax collectors doing that? And if you greet only your own people, what are you doing more than others? Do not even pagans do that? Be perfect, therefore, as your heavenly Father is perfect.

In another example of loving the enemy in *Uncle Tom's Cabin*, Eliza, the Shelby's runaway slave, is worried about what will happen to the slave catcher who tried to catch her and her son. When a few people see that Tom is struggling for life, she has the unselfish nature to say this:

"O, I hope he isn't killed!" said Eliza, who, with all the party, stood watching the proceeding.

"Why not?" said Phineas; "serves him right."

"Because, after death comes the judgement." Said Eliza.

"Yes," said the old woman, who had been groaning and praying in her Methodist fashion, during all the encounter, "it's an awful case for the poor crittur's soul."

Our first natural instinct when we face an enemy is to strike back and have no mercy. However, Eliza's faith in Jesus Christ is so strong that even in her most arduous moments that were caused by her enemy; she still has empathy for him. Where does empathy like that come from? Is it genetic? Is it evolutionary? Or does it come from a far greater power?

*

Even Robert Wright, who wrote the book, *Moral Animal*, claims that we are motivated in part by our own self-interest. He states:

Altruism, compassion, empathy, love, conscience, the sense of justice—all of these things, the things that hold society together, the things that allow our species to think so highly of itself, can now confidently be said to have a firm genetic basis. That's the good news. The bad news is that, although these things are in some ways blessings for humanity as a whole, they didn't evolve for the "good of the species" and aren't reliably employed to that end. Quite the contrary: it is now clearer than ever how (and precisely why) the moral sentiments are used with brutal flexibility, switched on and off in keeping with self-interest; and how naturally oblivious we often are to this switching. In the new view, human beings are a species splendid in their array of moral equipment, tragic in their propensity to misuse it, and pathetic in their constitutional ignorance of the misuse. The title of this book is not wholly without irony.

Wright, who grew up a Southern Baptist, is known today as an agnostic. He vehemently opposes creationism; he even opposes intelligent design. He would probably disagree with many portions of this book. However, even he talks about a brutal flexibility that is switched on and off in keeping with our self-interest. He claims as well that we are naturally oblivious to this switching. I would agree with this as well. Because of our selfishness and lack of natural empathy toward one another, we are oblivious to the effects of our actions on one another.

I believe that until we have some sort of religion or moral compass, we are oblivious to helping our fellow human beings unless it would help us out in the future. From an evolutionary standpoint, it clearly does not make sense to help our fellow being because we operate using the survival of the fittest mentality. Wright further talks about our propensity to misuse what we have. I would agree with him in that we misuse what we have because as Romans 3:23 so bluntly points out: "For all have sinned and fall short of the glory of God."

7

Mercy is Power

In many instances, it does not make sense for a human being to help out another fellow human being. From my standpoint, empathy *doesn't* come from science or happen by random chance. It happens ultimately because of that character's relationship with Jesus Christ. It is true that all of us are equal as Christians, and we cannot "earn" our way into heaven, but Jesus also tells us that in John 14:15: "If you love me, keep my commands." When we do keep his commandments by living out the Golden Rule, the recipient not only feels better, but we do as well.

*

All of us need help. Whether we are poor financially, poor in spirit, or poor in any other area, we all need help. But that help often comes at a hefty price. The best way to tell if someone is with you is to see whether a person will help you even if he knows he will get nothing in return from you. Anyone can help when there is something to gain in return; to help when there is nothing to be gained shows true love.

In Biblical times, there was a big difference between a "hired hand" and an actual shepherd. John 10:12 says, "the hired hand is not the shepherd and does not own the sheep. So when he sees the wolf coming, he abandons the sheep and runs away. Then the wolf attacks the flock and scatters it." Loving when there is something to get in return makes someone a "hired hand."

In *To Kill a Mockingbird,* the Cunningham's, a poor family, play an integral part of the book. Mr. Cunningham, who is Atticus's age, cannot afford to pay Atticus for the services he provides. Instead of demanding that he be paid, Atticus just says, "let that be the least of your worries." The mercy that Atticus shows him is very unlike this parable of the unmerciful servant found in Matthew 18:21–35.

Then Peter came to Jesus and asked, "Lord, how many times shall I forgive my brother or sister who sins against me? Up to seven times?" Jesus answered, "I tell you, not seven times, but seventy-seven times.

"Therefore, the kingdom of heaven is like a king who wanted to settle accounts with his servants. As he began the settlement, a man who owed him ten thousand bags of gold was brought to him. Since he was not able to pay, the master ordered that he and his wife and his children and all that he had be sold to repay the debt.

"At this the servant fell on his knees before him. 'Be patient with me,' he begged, 'and I will pay back everything.' The servant's master took pity on him, canceled the debt and let him go.

"But when that servant went out, he found one of his fellow servants who owed him a hundred silver coins. He grabbed him and began to choke him. 'Pay back what you owe me!' he demanded.

"His fellow servant fell to his knees and begged him, 'Be patient with me, and I will pay it back.'

"But he refused. Instead, he went off and had the man thrown into prison until he could pay the debt. When the other servants saw what had happened, they were outraged and went and told their master everything that had happened.

"Then the master called the servant in. 'You wicked servant,' he said, 'I canceled all that debt of yours because you begged me to. Shouldn't you have had mercy on your fellow servant just as I had on you?' In anger his master handed him over to the jailers to be tortured, until he should pay back all he owed.

"This is how my heavenly Father will treat each of you unless you forgive your brother or sister from your heart."

Showing mercy toward others is not an easy task. It requires patience, humility, and an inverse style of thinking that goes against our natural selfish desires. It also requires giving up a sense of control, a sense of control we often feel like we earned in the first place. It is important for human beings to consider if they are in a situation where they could dispense mercy to the person who gave them the power in the first place. If a person has made more money, who gave him the skills to make more money? If he has more intelligence, he needs to ask himself who gave him his wonderful brain. The answer to that question is simple: it was God. What God wants most to see is a person in power to give mercy to others just as God gave mercy to us when we were powerless.

Speaking of an inverse style of thinking and showing mercy to others, one of the most powerful passages in *Uncle Tom's Cabin* is the one below:

"I broke a fellow in, once," said St. Clare, "that all the overseers and masters had tried their hands on in vain."

"You!" said Marie; "well, I'd be glad to know when *you* ever did anything of the sort."

"Well, he was a powerful, gigantic fellow,—a native-born African; and he appeared to have the rude instinct of freedom in him to an uncommon degree. He was a regular African lion. They called him Scipio. Nobody could do anything with him; and he was sold round from overseer to overseer, till at last Alfred bought him, because he thought he could manage him. Well, one day he knocked down the overseer, and was fairly off into the swamps. I was on a visit to Alf's plantation, for it was after we had dissolved partnership. Alfred was greatly exasperated; but I told him that it was his own fault, and laid him any wager that I could break the man; and finally it was agreed that, if I caught him, I should have him to experiment on. So they mustered out a party of some six or seven, with guns and dogs, for the hunt. People, you know, can get up as much enthusiasm in hunting a man as a deer, if it is only customary; in fact, I got a little excited myself, though I had only put in as a sort of mediator, in case he was caught.

"Well, the dogs bayed and howled, and we rode and scampered, and finally we started him. He ran and bounded like a buck, and kept us well in the rear for some time; but at last he got caught in an impenetrable thicket of cane; then he turned to bay, and I tell you he fought the dogs right gallantly. He dashed them to right and left, and actually killed three of them with only his naked fists, when a shot from a gun brought him down, and he fell, wounded and bleeding, almost at my feet. The poor fellow looked up at me with manhood and despair both in his eye. I kept back the dogs and the party, as they came pressing up, and claimed him as my prisoner. It was all I could do to keep them from shooting him, in the flush of success; but I persisted in my bargain, and Alfred sold him to me. Well, I took him in hand, and in one fortnight I had him tamed down as submissive and tractable as heart could desire."

"What in the world did you do to him?" said Marie.

"Well, it was quite a simple process. I took him to my own room, had a good bed made for him, dressed his wounds, and tended him myself, until he got fairly on his feet again. And, in process of time, I had free papers made out for him, and told him he might go where he liked."

"And did he go?" said Miss Ophelia.

"No. The foolish fellow tore the paper in two, and absolutely refused to leave me. I never had a braver, better fellow,—trusty and true as steel. He embraced Christianity afterwards, and became as gentle as a child. He used to oversee my place on the lake, and did it capitally, too. I lost him the first cholera season. In fact, he laid down his life for me. For I was sick, almost to death; and when, through the panic, everybody else fled, Scipio worked for me like a giant, and actually brought me back into life again. But, poor fellow! he was taken, right after, and there was no saving him. I never felt anybody's loss more."

This sort of treatment of others has actually helped me out in my career of software sales. Rather than ramming the product down a customer's throat, I have been honest with them from the on-set of our relationship. That inverse style of thinking helped me close a seven-figure deal off of a cold call while I was working at a start-up. It works in part because of the rarity in it. It was rare that I treated my prospects with the Golden Rule, and because I did so, they were quick to listen to me and even quicker to trust me.

*

Every once in a while, you run into a person who has every right to make you feel inferior. He might have more money or status than you. He might be smarter than you or possess significantly more talent than you. There are plenty of people who you run into that let you know that they have the power of you. Regardless of how many people there are like that, there a select few who make you feel like you too can be like them and that you too can feel special. You begin to forget all of your insecurities, lose all inhibitions; they make you feel equal to them. In their dealing with you, it is so rare because you realize all the power they have is distributed equally like 30 minutes in an hour glass.

In *To Kill a Mockingbird*, the Finches, and Atticus in particular, had that effect on the younger Cunningham. Jem and Scout are headed home and Jem decides that it is OK to take young Walter back with so he can have a full meal for a change. Walter is certainly "less" than the Finches on the social and economic ladder. At one point later in the novel, Aunt Alexandra, who thinks that their family is better than everybody, encourages Scout that she should not bring Walter home. She tells Scout: "I didn't say not to be nice to him. You should be friendly and polite to him, you should be gracious to everybody, dear. But you don't have to invite him home." Anyhow, even though Walter usually wouldn't feel welcome in a home like the Finches, he did after the way Scout and Jem treat him.

Jem does invite Walter over for supper eventually. After school, Jem and Scout who are more upper-class walk to the Finches with Walter who is of more lower-class. They must have had an effect on Walter because the narrator writes that "by the time we reached our front steps, Walter had forgotten he was a Cunningham."

When Walter finally does come to the Finches, they treat him to supper. He does a strange thing when he eats however. He drowns all of his dinner in syrup. Scout has no idea how to respond.

What Calpurnia teaches Scout after is the highest form of Southern hospitality:

"There's some folks who don't eat like us," she whispered fiercely, "but you ain't called on to contradict 'em at the table when they don't. That boy's yo' comp'ny and if he wants to eat up the table cloth you let him, your hear?"

"He ain't company, Cal, he's just a Cunningham—"

"Hush your mouth! Don't matter who they are, anybody that sets foot in this house's yo' comp'ny, and don't you let me catch you remarkin' on their ways like you was so high and mighty! Yo' folks might be btter'n the Cunninghams but it don't count for disgrac' the way you're disgracing' 'em if you can't act fit to eat at the table you can just set here and eat in the kitchen."

Calpurnia has an interesting point. If the Finches were truly better than the Cunningham's, then why did Scout feel as if she had to rub it in Walter's face? Shouldn't she feel secure enough in her own heart not to look down on him? Again, it comes down to the manner in which she enjoys certain advantages over others, and in this instance, she did not enjoy them with grace.

*

Similar scenes occur in *Uncle Tom's Cabin* as well. Miss Ophelia, who is Eva's aunt, comes down to the South with an air of moral superiority because she believes in the complete abolition of slavery. She constantly debates her relative St. Clare over the issue because of her faith rooted in Christianity. St. Clare wants to see what her real intentions were with the slaves and places Topsy, an absolute troublemaker of a child, in her care. Topsy had been abused in her last home and is always making mischief and being naughty. Eva implores her to start behaving:

"What does make you so bad, Topsy? Why won't you try and be good? Don't you love anybody, Topsy?"

"Donno nothing 'bout love; I loves candy and sich, that's all," said Topsy.

"But you love your father and mother?"

"Never had none, ye know. I telled ye that, Miss Eva."

"O, I know," said Eva, sadly; "but hadn't you any brother, or sister, or aunt, or—"

"No, none on 'em,—never had nothing nor nobody."

"But, Topsy, if you'd only try to be good, you might—"

"Couldn't never be nothin' but a nigger, if I was ever so good," said Topsy. "If I could be skinned, and come white, I'd try then."

"But people can love you, if you are black, Topsy. Miss Ophelia would love you, if you were good."

Topsy gave the short, blunt laugh that was her common mode of expressing incredulity.

"Don't you think so?" said Eva.

"No; she can't bar me, 'cause I'm a nigger!—she'd 's soon have a toad touch her! There can't nobody love niggers, and niggers can't do nothin'! I don't care," said Topsy, beginning to whistle.

"O, Topsy, poor child, I love you!" said Eva, with a sudden burst of feeling, and laying her little thin, white hand on Topsy's shoulder; "I love you, because you haven't had any father, or mother, or friends;—because you've been a poor, abused child! I love you, and I want you to be good. I am very unwell, Topsy, and I think I shan't live a great while; and it really grieves me, to have you be so naughty. I wish you would try to be good, for my sake;— it's only a little while I shall be with you."

The round, keen eyes of the black child were over-cast with tears;—large, bright drops rolled heavily down, one by one, and fell on the little white hand. Yes, in that moment, a ray of real belief, a ray of heavenly love, had penetrated the darkness of her heathen soul! She laid her head down between her knees, and wept and sobbed,—while the beautiful child, bending over her, looked like the picture of some bright angel stooping to reclaim a sinner.

"Poor Topsy!" said Eva, "don't you know that Jesus loves all alike? He is just as willing to love you, as me. He loves you just as I do,—only more, because he is better. He will help you to be good; and you can go to Heaven at last, and be an angel forever, just as much as if you were white. Only think of it, Topsy!—you can be one of those spirits bright, Uncle Tom sings about."

"O, dear Miss Eva, dear Miss Eva!" said the child; "I will try, I will try; I never did care nothin' about it before."

St. Clare, at this instant, dropped the curtain. "It puts me in mind of mother," he said to Miss Ophelia. "It is true what she told me; if we want to give sight to the blind, we must be willing to do as Christ did,—call them to us, and put our hands on them."

"I've always had a prejudice against negroes," said Miss Ophelia, "and it's a fact, I never could bear to have that child touch me; but, I don't think she knew it."

"Trust any child to find that out," said St. Clare; "there's no keeping it from them. But I believe that all the trying in the world to benefit a child, and all the substantial favors you can do them, will never excite one emotion of gratitude, while that feeling of repugnance remains in the heart;—it's a queer kind of a fact,—but so it is."

"I don't know how I can help it," said Miss Ophelia; "they are disagreeable to me,—this child in particular,—how can I help feeling so?"

"Eva does, it seems."

"Well, she's so loving! After all, though, she's no more than Christ-like," said Miss Ophelia; "I wish I were like her. She might teach me a lesson."

"It wouldn't be the first time a little child had been used to instruct an old disciple, if it were so," said St. Clare.

8

Pretended Patriotism

One can tell when another person loves him or not. Maya Angelou once said, "I've learned that people will forget what you said, people will forget what you did, but people will never forget how you made them feel." Ophelia refused to actually *touch* Topsy, and kids are inherently smart enough to know whether someone is truly on their side. The definition of touch is pretty simple: "come so close to (an object) as to be or come into contact with." Thus, one cannot touch someone or something unless they mean to come into contact with that other object. In other words, it takes effort to touch someone else. But if one is intimate with another person, they will not be afraid them.

*

George Washington once stated: "Guard against the impostures of pretended patriotism." Pretended patriotism is exactly what Miss Ophelia is guilty of. Sure, she offers to help Topsy out, but she never intends to treat her like a human being. What she was doing was actually worse than whipping the child. Hypocrisy is the worst type of sin because it puts Christianity in a bad light. It assumes piety but it is really just the opposite of it.

In an op-ed published in 2008 in the *Washington Post*, Amelia Rawls describes the types of people like Ophelia in a piece that dealt with Ivy League students:

During four years at Princeton University and nearly a year at Yale Law School, I have been surrounded by students who dazzle. These are the students for whom application processes were made. They include published novelists, acclaimed musicians and Olympic medalists. They include entrepreneurs, founders of human rights groups and political activists. If they have hobbies such as stamp collecting and belly dancing, by golly, they are the best stamp collectors and belly dancers in America! These youths live a life of superlatives, a life in which being No. 1 is not just an aspiration but the status quo. They can be inspirational, and I am lucky to be able to learn from them. But they are not always nice people.

You know what I mean by "nice." I mean the kind of "nice" that involves showing compassion not merely because membership in community service groups demands it. The kind of "nice" that involves sharing notes with a student who is sick or lending a textbook to a friend who doesn't have one. The kind of selfless, genuine "nice" that makes this world a better place—but won't get you accepted to college.

Of course, top universities accept hundreds of individuals who have demonstrated the highest levels of citizenship. These teenagers have volunteered in more food banks, sponsored more fundraisers and lobbied more officials than any previous generation. They earn, rightfully, the gratitude of their communities and the plethora of honors that come with it. Colleges at the top of *U.S. News and World Report*'s rankings would balk at the notion that these students are anything but the best and the brightest.

I'm not saying different. I'm saying that sometimes some of these students will denounce world hunger but be unfriendly to the homeless. They will debate environmental policy but never offer to take out the trash. They will believe vehemently in many causes but roll their eyes when reminded to be humble, to be generous and to "do what is right."

Just as Rawls points out the hypocrisy that goes on at Ivy League schools, Topsy also points out to Eva that Miss Ophelia would rather touch a toad than touch her. Deep love has no selfish angles, no contrived messages. It operates rather on a sense of selflessness, a sense of selflessness that conveys forgetting one's needs for a minute and focusing on the needs of others. It's the type of love that makes this world a better place.

Speaking of the world, as mentioned before, God often tells us that being of the world is of no use. This is not so easy for us to do, however, because of how we are hardwired as human beings. In *David and Goliath*, Malcom Gladwell explains this in full:

Innovators have to be open. They have to be able to imagine things that others cannot and to be willing to challenge their own preconceptions. They also need to be conscientious. An innovator who has brilliant ideas but lacks the discipline and persistence to carry them out is merely a dreamer. That, too, is obvious.

But crucially, innovators need to be *dis*agreeable. By disagreeable, I don't mean obnoxious or unpleasant. I mean that on the 5th dimension of the Big Five personality inventory, "agreeableness," they are people willing to take *social* risks—to do things that others might disapprove of.

That is not easy. Society frowns upon disagreeableness. As human beings we are hardwired to seek the approval of those around us. Yet a radical and transformative thought goes nowhere without the willingness to challenge convention. "If you have a new idea, and it's disruptive and you're agreeable, then what are you going to do with that?" says psychologist Jordan Peterson. "If you worry about hurting people's feelings and disturbing the social structure, you're not going to put your ideas forward." As the playwright George Bernard Shaw once put it: "The reasonable man adapts himself to the world: the unreasonable one persists in trying to adopt the world to himself. Therefore all progress depends on the unreasonable man."

In order to live how God would want us to live, we have to be disagreeable. Being disagreeable on a day-to-day basis is one of the hardest things to do in life. I can think of many times in my own life when I have tried to be agreeable to others to please them and in doing so have turned my back on God. There is a line from *The Great Gatsby* that is one of my favorites. Jay Gatsby was such a great character because of his disagreeableness.

He smiled understandingly—much more than understandingly. It was one of those rare smiles with a quality of eternal reassurance in it, that you may come across four or five times in life. It faced—or seemed to face—the whole eternal world for an instant, and then concentrated on you with an irresistible prejudice in your favor. It understood you just as far as you wanted to be understood, believed in you as you would like to believe in yourself, and assured you that it had precisely the impression of you that, at your best, you hoped to convey.

This is how Christ looks at us even in our sin and is exactly how we should look at others.

*

So many times, whether we mean it or not, we are just like Scout in the instance with the Cunningham's; we demean others in one way or another. We have no right to do this because we are all made in the image of God. All of us are equal under God's eyes whether we are the CEO of a company, a homeless person on the street, or have some sort of developmental disability.

In my own life, the most pronounced time this happened to me occurred through a communication I had through email with the CEO of SAP, Bill McDermott, one of the most respected business software companies in the world. I had reached out to the CEO with a LinkedIn message and an email telling him why he should hire a 25-year-old to be VP of Lead Generation, which is essentially head of inside sales or cold calling. To my delight, he responded. He got me in touch with a recruiter as well. I didn't end up getting the job, but it was still a really neat connection to have made.

Months later, he had a horrible freak accident and actually ended up losing an eye. I felt badly for him, so I sent him a favorite quote of mine from Thomas Paine:

> The harder the conflict, the more glorious the triumph. What we obtain too cheap, we esteem too lightly; it is dearness only that gives everything its value. I love the man that can smile in trouble, that can gather strength from distress and grow brave by reflection. 'Tis the business of little minds to shrink; but he whose heart is firm, and whose conscience approves his conduct, will pursue his principles unto death.

To my surprise, he not only responded but responded within two and a half hours. I have encountered people in my own life who always say they are too busy to get back to me, and here is the CEO of a $95 billion company who responded within an hour and a half. I was no longer just a 25-year-old kid who made cold calls for a living. He made me feel as if I were his equal. I was no longer a Cunningham.

I have kept in touch with him mainly through his communications aid, Nick Tzizon. Nick has given me career advice from time to time and serves as a great mentor to me. In June of 2017 I emailed Bill letting him know that I had gotten my first real taste of management at my current company. Even though it was on a Saturday morning, he responded within about two hours later from his phone with "Great job Thomas!!! You can get anything you want in this world if you help enough other people get what they want. All the satisfaction in leadership comes from helping others achieve their dreams." At the time, SAP had a market cap of over $133 Billion and over 80,000 employees.

On SAP's Diversity and Recruitment page, McDermott says, "Our vision is to help the world run better and improve people's lives. This means the entire world and all people. We do not limit our purpose by country, color or creed. Let's challenge ourselves to be a unifying force, especially in those moments when our raw emotions tempt otherwise. Let our only bias be for trust, the ultimate human currency. We don't need permission to make this difference, only compassion, an open mind and a heart full of love." As great as this sounds, has McDermott actually followed through on his words? Absolutely. In May 2013 SAP launched its Autism at Work program which focuses on bringing people on the autism spectrum into the workplace at SAP. Although autism is a disability, there are many strengths that the disorder brings to the table at a technology company like SAP. Jose Velasco, head of the program, explains how SAP takes initiatives to train people: "It's an additional four-to-six-week, scenario-based program that focuses on soft skills, communication, teamwork, meeting etiquette, e-mail etiquette and disability disclosure. When an employee on the spectrum comes into SAP, they have access to these job and life-skills programs if they need it."

Whether people admit it in the clergy or other nonprofits, I have sometimes seen them have an attitude of disdain for people in the business world. While this way of thinking may have some merit at times for the greedy and power-hungry conduct of some business people, McDermott shows that this is not always the case.

*

In *To Kill a Mockingbird*, Boo Radley is the most mysterious character of all. All three children make it their quest to see him in person one day. Even though they are scared of him and even make fun of him, he is the one at the end of the novel that saves their lives when they are coming home from the Halloween festival. To understand Boo Radley's role in the book is to understand the theme of *To Kill a Mockingbird* overall. The book, as well as our lives, depends on the unselfishness and understanding of one another. When Scout gets into bed that night after both children were attacked, she reads a book with Atticus called "The Gray Ghost." It took her until the end of the books to understand it's meaning however: "An' they chased him 'n' never could catch him 'cause they didn't know what he looked like, an' Atticus, when they finally saw him, why he hadn't done any of those things … Atticus, he was real nice." Atticus's response was simple: "Most people are, Scout, when you finally see them."

The question that is posed to us is do we have to wait until the end of the book to understand people, or will we have the foresight to crawl into someone's skin and walk around in it right away?

*

Holding someone accountable for their actions can be one of the most delicate and awkward dealing that a human being has to do for another. But in strong relationships, this happens frequently. Proverbs 27:17 says, "As iron sharpens iron, so one person sharpens another." If someone truly loves you as a friend, he will sacrifice the awkward moment that comes with criticizing you and do so. If he does not think that you are capable of change, however, or does not think it is worth his effort, he will say nothing.

This same thing occurs in *Uncle Tom's Cabin* when Tom notices that his master St. Clare is not living up to his full potential. St. Clare sees that he is very sad and says:

"Why, Tom, what's the case? You look as solemn as a coffin."

"I feel very bad, Mas'r. I always have thought that Mas'r would be good to everybody."

"Well, Tom, haven't I been? Come, now, what do yon want?"

"Mas'r allays been good to me. I haven't nothing to complain of, on that head. But there is one that Mas'r isn't good to."

"Why, Tom, what's got into you? Speak out; what do you mean?"

"Last night, between one and two, I thought so. I studied upon the matter then. Mas'r isn't good to himself."

St. Clare felt his face flush crimson, but he laughed. "Oh, that's all, is it?" he said, gayly.

"All!" said Tom, turning suddenly round, and falling, on his knees. "O, my dear young, Mas'r! I'm 'fraid it will be loss of all— all—body and—soul. The good Book says, 'it biteth like a serpent and stingeth like an adder!' my dear Mas'r!"

Tom's voice choked and the tears ran down his cheeks.

"You poor, silly fool!" said St. Clare, with tears in his own eyes. "Get up, Tom. I'm not worth crying over."

Hebrews 12:4–12 goes on to say that,

> In your struggle against sin, you have not yet resisted to the point of shedding your blood. And have you completely forgotten this word of encouragement that addresses you as a father addresses his son?

> My son, do not make light of the Lord's discipline, and do not lose heart when he rebukes you, because the Lord disciplines the one he loves, and he chastens everyone he accepts as his son." Endure hardship as discipline; God is treating you as his children. For what children are not disciplined by their

father? If you are not disciplined—and everyone undergoes discipline—then you are not legitimate, not true sons and daughters at all. Moreover, we have all had human fathers who disciplined us and we respected them for it. How much more should we submit to the Father of spirits and live! They disciplined us for a little while as they thought best; but God disciplines us for our good, in order that we may share in his holiness. No discipline seems pleasant at the time, but painful. Later on, however, it produces a harvest of righteousness and peace for those who have been trained by it. Therefore, strengthen your feeble arms and weak knees. "Make level paths for your feet," so that the lame may not be disabled, but rather healed.

So many times, we lash out against others when they give us advice or critique our actions. We need to realize they are doing so because they believe in us and think we are capable of greatness. The real time to question your actions is when everyone is silent. Living out the Golden Rule to others means constantly putting yourself in positions that help others. One of the most important positions you can put yourself is in the position to politely critique one's actions if they are not pleasing to the Lord.

*

The aspect that makes Eva so angelic throughout *Uncle Tom's Cabin* is her reactions to certain situations. Place a person in certain situations and see how they react whether those situations be adverse or positive. That is how you can tell one's true character. At one point in the book there is a quote that is the essence of true empathy and living out the Golden Rule. The quote is "any mind that is capable of *real sorrow* is capable of good." We have to ask ourselves the question what is real sorrow. Is real sorrow stepping on the scale and realizing we gained 10 pounds in the last winter? Is real sorrow realizing that we didn't get the raise needed in order to move to a prestigious address? No, these are not all examples of real sorrow. Real sorrow is putting yourself in another's shoes at a time of distress and weeping alongside them. Real sorrow is putting others' emotions ahead of your own emotion. Real sorrow has none of the selfishness that is inextricably bound to our souls from birth.

Eva constantly does this throughout the book. At one point, Tom tells Eva of a slave who turned to drinking due to her problems that she faced because she was a slave: "Tom, in simple, earnest phrase, told Eva the history of a poor slave rusk-woman whose last child had been taken from her, and who was drinking herself to death in order to drown her misery. Eva did not exclaim, or wonder, or weep, as other children do. Her cheeks grew pale, and a deep, earnest shadow passed over her eyes. She laid both hands on her bosom, and sighed heavily."

9

Becoming Christlike

It's been widely known and acknowledged that the best way to turn someone over to Jesus is not just by merely trying to convert them on your own but to show them the way by acting like Christ toward them and others. I went to Samford University, a Baptist-affiliated school in the South. At one point, I had a friend who would literally go up to people in malls and ask them if they knew Jesus. If I were a recipient of this, not only would I be deeply disturbed but also deeply offended. I would think who is he to tell me that he is right and I am wrong?

In *Uncle Tom's Cabin*, Tom is much more effective at showing the gospel to others by his *actions*, not his *words*. Toward the end of the book, the narrator describes the effect that Tom has had on his fellow slaves:

> Tom's whole soul overflowed with compassion and sympathy for the poor wretches by whom he was surrounded. To him it seemed as if his life-sorrows were now over, and as if, out of that strange treasury of peace and joy, with which he had been endowed from above, he longed to pour out something

for the relief of their woes. It is true, opportunities were scanty; but, on the way to the fields, and back again, and during the hours of labor, chances fell in his way of extending a helping-hand to the weary, the disheartened and discouraged. The poor, worn-down, brutalized creatures, at first, could scarce comprehend this; but, when it was continued week after week, and month after month, it began to awaken long-silent chords in their benumbed hearts. Gradually and imperceptibly the strange, silent, patient man, who was ready to bear every one's burden, and sought help from none,—who stood aside for all, and came last, and took least, yet was foremost to share his little all with any who needed,—the man who, in cold nights, would give up his tattered blanket to add to the comfort of some woman who shivered with sickness, and who filled the baskets of the weaker ones in the field, at the terrible risk of coming short in his own measure,—and who, though pursued with unrelenting cruelty by their common tyrant, never joined in uttering a word of reviling or cursing,—this man, at last, began to have a strange power over them; and, when the more pressing season was past, and they were allowed again their Sundays for their own use, many would gather together to hear from him of Jesus. They would gladly have met to hear, and pray, and sing, in some place, together; but Legree would not permit it, and more than once broke up such attempts, with oaths and brutal execrations,— so that the blessed news had to circulate from individual to individual.

Actions speak louder than words because actions take effort. Saying you will do something is one thing, but actually following through on it is another.

*

James 2:14-26 states that faith without works is dead. While people vehemently argue over what exactly this may mean, we could easily be missing the point of the passage. What people argue about in this verse is the fact that all people are equal as Christians in the Bible, so they cannot have enough works to put you in the right standing with God. As mentioned before, Jesus often tells us that you only love him unless you obey his commandments. Here is the passage from James below:

What does it profit, my brethren, if someone says he has faith but does not have works? Can faith save him? If a brother or sister is naked and destitute of daily food, and one of you says to them, "Depart in peace, be warmed and filled," but you do not give them the things which are needed for the body, what does it profit? Thus also faith by itself, if it does not have works, is dead. But someone will say, "You have faith, and I have works." Show me your faith without your works, and I will show you my faith by my works. You believe that there is one God. You do well. Even the demons believe—and tremble! But do you want to know, O foolish man, that faith without works is dead? Was not Abraham our father justified by works when he offered Isaac his son on the altar? Do you see that faith was working together with his works, and by works faith was made perfect? And the Scripture was fulfilled which says, "Abraham believed God, and it was accounted to him for righteousness." And he was called the friend of God. You see then that a man is justified by works, and not by faith only.

Likewise, was not Rahab the harlot also justified by works when she received the messengers and sent them out another way? For as the body without the spirit is dead, so faith without works is dead also.

Perhaps James was wondering how others are going to be converted to Christianity if they do not see an outside change? I've already mentioned a quote by Bada Gara mentioning that Christian's aren't Christ like. While this is certainly the case because humans are naturally sinful, for non-Christians to see the reason to join a faith there must be some natural consistency to it. This could be exactly why Paul wrote this in the Bible. At the very least, it is an interesting way to look at it.

In my own life, I have been disappointed to see people proclaiming to love Christ and be a strong Christian when they did not live out the Golden Rule. It actually made me question some of my own decisions because I was, in effect, questioning the power of Christianity. I experienced a moral dilemma involving a friend and knew what my friend would do but questioned his real intentions. After numerous phone calls and texts went unanswered, I became fed up with him and almost made the bad moral mistake. The person who convince me to do the right think after all was a friend who was considered less devout (i.e., he drank heavily in college at times). He was able to convince me to do the right thing because he had invested more in me because he had lived out the Golden Rule.

*

There's a good example of this in *Uncle Tom's Cabin* when Tom is able to woo the overseers, who were formally nasty men, into wanting to become Christians.

Yet Tom was not quite gone. His wondrous words and pious prayers had struck upon the hearts of the imbruted blacks, who had been the instruments of cruelty upon him; and, the instant Legree withdrew, they took him down, and, in their ignorance, sought to call him back to life,—as if that were any favor to him.

"Sartin, we 's been doin' a dreffful wicked thing!" said Sambo; "hopes Mas'r 'll have to 'count for it, and not we."

They washed his wounds,—they provided a rude bed, of some refuse cotton, for him to lie down on; and one of them, stealing up to the house, begged a drink of brandy of Legree, pretending that he was tired, and wanted it for himself. He brought it back, and poured it down Tom's throat.

"O, Tom!" said Quimbo, "we's been awful wicked to ye!"

"I forgive ye, with all my heart!" said Tom, faintly.

"O, Tom! do tell us who is Jesus, anyhow?" said Sambo;—"Jesus, that's been a standin' by you so, all this night!—Who is he?"

The word roused the failing, fainting spirit. He poured forth a few energetic sentences of that wondrous One,—his life, his death, his everlasting presence, and power to save.

They wept,—both the two savage men.

"Why didn't I never hear this before?" said Sambo; "but I do believe!—I can't help it! Lord Jesus, have mercy on us!"

"Poor critters!" said Tom, "I'd be willing to bar' all I have, if it'll only bring ye to Christ! O, Lord! give me these two more souls, I pray!"

That prayer was answered!

*

Another example of Tom changing the culture of a place around him can be found when Tom first got to Simon Legree's place. You could even say that his actions shocked others:

Tom waited till a late hour, to get a place at the mills; and then, moved by the utter weariness of two women, whom he saw trying to grind their corn there, he ground for them, put together the decaying brands of the fire, where many had baked cakes before them, and then went about getting his own supper. It was a new kind of work there,—a deed of charity, small as it was; but it woke an answering touch in their hearts,—an expression of womanly kindness came over their hard faces; they mixed his cake for him, and tended its baking; and Tom sat down by the light of the fire, and drew out his Bible,—for he had need of comfort.

We all need an "answering touch" in our hearts, and the only way we get it is when other people live out the Golden Rule onto us. When we witness people living the Golden Rule, it gives us hope because it is uncommon for someone to do that unto us. It shows us that people are actually on our side and care for us. It's an elementary tenet in the Christian way of life, but one that often gets lost in how some people profess the faith.

You can tell a lot about a person by their last words. People rarely say they wished they worked longer hours or made more money; they talk about wishing they spent more time with their loved ones. Tom was the same way but even more slightly adamant about not just loving his family, but loving *everyone*. He says, "'Pears like I love 'em all. I loves every crittur, everywhar!—it's nothing *but* love! O, Mas'r George! What a thing 'tis to be a Christian!"

Just imagine if everyone in the world, including you, was wired this way. We would have no war, no one would ever go hungry, and we would truly all care for each other.

Children often take after their parents in the way they treat other people. As I mentioned earlier in the situation with my father, he has passed down many positive traits to me in being kind to those who are in a "lower status" than we are. In *Uncle Tom's Cabin* Eva is introduced Henrique, her slightly older cousin. Like Eva's mother, Henrique is slightly mystified as to how Eva treats the slaves. At one point, Eva calls Henrique out for the way he treats the slaves. Henrique then changes his tune and becomes nicer to the slave whom he treated poorly but not as thoughtful as Eva: "And Henrique cantered down the walk after Eva. Dodo stood looking after the two children. One had given him money; and one had given him what he wanted far more,—a kind word, kindly spoken."

People who are in a "lower" status than someone who is above them cherish nothing more than one thing from that other person: to be treated equally. Giving tips and advice can actually be demeaning to them. Equality is an important concept to those in a "lower" status.

Henrique again falls into the same line of thinking that many characters in *To Kill a Mockingbird* and *Uncle Tom's Cabin* fall. They claim to treat people equally, but they don't really mean this fully. Here is an example below from *Uncle Tom's Cabin*:

"Would you think you were well off, if there were not one creature in the world near you to love you?"

"I? Well, of course not."

"And you have taken Dodo away from all the friends he ever had, and now he has not a creature to love him; nobody can be good that way."

"Well, I can't help it, as I know of. I can't get his mother, and I can't love him myself, nor anybody else, as I know of."

"Why can't you?" said Eva.

"Love Dodo! Why, Eva, you wouldn't have me! I may like him well enough; but you don't love your servants."

"I do, indeed."

"How odd!"

"Don't the Bible say we must love everybody?"

Again, Eva is called out by a character for being *odd*. Oftentimes, as humans we shy away from the words peculiar, uncommon, strange, or odd when we should really be drawn to those characteristics. The reason for this is because the sacrifice that Christ made for us on the cross was all of these words and more. We don't deserve to be united with him because of our sin but we are because of his love for us.

*

Eva's love for others is just like Christ's and Atticus's in the fact that it transcends all understanding. Here is another example of that: "I can't tell you; but, when I saw those poor creatures on the boat,

104

you know, when you came up and I,—some had lost their mothers, and some their husbands, and some mothers cried for their little children,—and when I heard about poor Prue,—oh, wasn't that dreadful!—and a great many other times, I've felt that I would be glad to die, if my dying could stop all this misery. I would die for them, Tom, if I could," said the child, earnestly, laying her little thin hand on his.

Most people would die for their friends or family, but someone who is willing to lay down his life for a complete stranger shows a different kind of love, a type of love that does not get any fuller. It's that type of love that believes all human life is precious, equal.

Kissing

Kissing is one of those things that prove that God really exists. Whether it is just a kiss on the cheek in friendship or a romantic kiss, we can all admit that they are special. Sweet Eva knew this, but she did not know that some people would see this as strange and odd.

"O, there's Mammy!" said Eva, as she flew across the room; and, throwing herself into her arms, she kissed her repeatedly.

This woman did not tell her that she made her head ache, but, on the contrary, she hugged her, and laughed, and cried, till her sanity was a thing to be doubted of; and when released from her, Eva flew from one to another, shaking hands and kissing, in a way that Miss Ophelia afterwards declared fairly turned her stomach.

"Well!" said Miss Ophelia, "you southern children can do something that I couldn't."

"What, now, pray?" said St. Clare.

"Well, I want to be kind to everybody, and I wouldn't have anything hurt; but as to kissing—"

"Niggers," said St. Clare, "that you're not up to,—hey?"

Kissing someone is a very personal form of contact. When I was at Samford, I had a similar experience with a cafeteria lady named Sonya. She was a young African American grandmother who had a distinctive golden tooth and plenty of sass. She would eventually become my surrogate mother in college. Just like Eva, I would give her a big kiss on the cheek every single time I saw her at the register. We did get strange looks on several occasions. People were probably wondering why a preppy white kid at a private school was kissing what they would think was just a cafeteria worker making minimum wage. In my mind however, we were both just human beings made in the image of God.

*

Our natural inclination is to think of ourselves first and foremost. The reason I think this is true is because I have thought this thought every day for the last 28 years of my life. Furthermore, in the *New York Times* bestseller *Thinking Fast and Thinking Slow*, Daniel Kahneman argues that there are two modes of thinking, System 1 and System 2. System 1 is fast, intuitive, and emotional. System 2 is slower, more deliberative, and more logical. Kahneman repeatedly states that we are naturally in the state of System 1. He also says that "people who are cognitively busy are also more likely to make selfish choices." In other words, we are naturally selfish. I too often think and stress about how work is going because I want money to spend on this or that to make myself feel materialistically comfortable. Rather, the proper focus needs to be on providing value to our customers or those who buy our products or services. By providing value to my customers, I too will benefit from being successful in my work.

Eva, instead of focusing on what she has going well for her in her life, is drawn to other's misfortunes as a cat is drawn to a mouse. Look how happy she is throughout the novel. Look at how she lives life. No word she speaks is wrong; everything she does lifts other people up. Until we start to live like Eva, we will never understand the purpose of life. At one point Eva worries about what will happen to all of the slaves. Her mother, Marie, comforts her, but it is of no use:

"Well, we can't help it; it's no use worrying, Eva! I don't know what's to be done; we ought to be thankful for our own advantages."

"I hardly can be," said Eva, "I'm so sorry to think of poor folks that haven't any."

To have that level of unselfishness is uncommon, but it produces a more fulfilling life for those people who live by it. There is always going to be a need to resolve one's own problems, but focusing on others has a pronounced, beneficial effect on the other person and one's own life.

*

The influence of Eva's ways even had a pronounced impact on Aunt Ophelia.

"Topsy, you poor child," she said, as she lead her into her room, "don't give up! I can love you, though I am not like that dear little child. I hope I've learned something of the love of Christ from her. I can love you; I do, and I'll try to help you to grow up a good Christian girl."

Miss Ophelia's voice was more than her words, and more than that were the honest tears that fell down on her face. From that hour, she acquired an influence over the mind of the destitute child that she never lost."

It is interesting how some attempt to have influence over others. Some try by force, which can work temporarily, but oftentimes does not have the same loyalty that one can garner by simply living out the Golden Rule to one another.

*

Tom says it in the simplest when he tells St. Clare that "we does for the Lord when we does for his critturs." They are simple words, but it is incredible to think how much better of a place the world would be if we lived by these words.

From my own life, I have been the happiest when I give back to others. Luckily, my father realized this as well and helped me out when I was in a bind. In May 2014, I made one of the stupidest decisions in my life. I invested in a penny stock and would lose thousands of dollars in a day and a half. I was at an SAP conference in Orlando and became very depressed. I had so much shame and embarrassment and I nearly lost all hope. I contemplated going to the hospital but did not. I received a few encouraging texts from my brother Chris that kept me afloat. When I arrived back in Atlanta I told my dad the news, my father was very disappointed and angry when I told him the decision I made. He took a direct shift in his attitude when I told him how low I was.

He immediately began to think of things to encourage me, and he reminded me the primary reason for life is to give back to others, not make money. There was an event coming up called the Southern Shindig that he said I should get involved with. The event was a fund-raiser for an organization that was a rehabilitation place for people with mental health issues. It was great for me to get involved in the event. It reminded me that life was not about me; it was about others. When we do for others, we provide more happiness for ourselves more effectively than when we try to focus only on ourselves. The reason for this is simple: putting ourselves in another's shoes makes us forget all about our own problems.

CONCLUSION

At one point in *To Kill a Mockingbird*, Miss Maudie remarks that people "in their right minds never take pride in their own talents." However noble this might seem, it actually only seems logical because we are not given our talents to begin with, they are given from above. Furthermore, they are given to us to be used to help people around us, not just help ourselves. It is a different way to look at life when you realize that what you have been given was meant to help your fellow man and not just yourself. Tim Keller once said, "every gift is also a duty."

*

What happens when we focus less on ourselves and instead devote that energy toward others? We benefit others and also benefit ourselves. When we reach out to someone who is in need, we fulfill the words of Christ. By following the Golden Rule in our attitude, behavior, and conduct, we make the world a better place and make our own lives better too.

No one said it would be easy to live out the Golden Rule. It is one of the toughest endeavors that a human being can set out to do. As mentioned earlier many times, we are very selfish from the day we are born. In *To Kill a Mockingbird*, Miss Maudie when speaking of Atticus says, "I simply want to tell you that there are some men in this world who were born to do our unpleasant jobs for us. Your father's one of them." You only love someone when you are willing to sacrifice for them; without sacrifice, there is no love.

EPILOGUE

Why I Should Be Considered

I believe I should be considered for a scholarship this year because I take pride in trying to live out the core values of the Brock School of Business. As elementary as it sounds, a genuine look into separate meanings of words in phrases reveals just how important they are, or should be.

For instance, what does the phrase *core value* mean to The Brock School of Business and do I ever embody it? For myself, when thinking about the word *core*, I think of something being strong and genuine. Since it is tough to get down to the core of anything; it is not always plain to see the core. At one point in the semester during Managerial Accounting with Dr. Belski it was tough to find my core… I had just made a raw 47 on a test, a test where he had written one of the most demoralizing things a teacher could write: *Thomas, we need to get you a tutor.* Anyway, we discussed a game plan for the rest of the semester and he said that "I would make it through his class." Although I appreciated his words, I wanted something more. I told him that I wasn't just worried about making it through the class, I was much more worried about using the information I learn now in 15 years if the chance ever came up in a real-world setting. I ended up getting SGA President and future PWC intern Sam Dickerson to tutor and certainly achieved some source of success in the class, achieving a B in it as a non-accounting major.

Unfortunately though, however heartwarming this story is, does it truly add any *value* to society? For instance, has the story above achieved any part of this frank core value listed on The Brock School of Business website? "We value the timely, relevant, participatory and experimental learning environments that develop well-trained persons who add value and achieve fulfilling roles within their organizations, communities, and the global environment." Not yet, for I was only well-trained. However, this past January I realized what it meant to actually add *value* to the community even it was only few employees at a local BBQ restaurant who had been treated illegally and unfairly by their boss.

Over MLK Jr. Break, I stopped by myself to grab a late lunch at a local BBQ restaurant in Anniston, AL on my way from Birmingham to Atlanta. Since the waitress wasn't too busy, we started to talk for a while. We continued to talk and somewhere down the line she complained to me that she was only being paid $2.13 an hour. Of course, minimum wage is $7.25, but a tipped employee can make less than this. I remembered from Belski's class the law required the boss to cover the additional money to get the wage up to the minimum wage if the tips did not cover it in an hour. Instead of doing this, the manager let the employees keep all of their tips and report 10% of their sales to the government in order to account for their tips.

When the waitress told me all of this, I started to wonder if she was getting treated unfairly, and I asked for a pen to write down some figures on a napkin. I then asked for some paper and was given a long receipt on which I wrote down my calculations and got this law or some variation of it off my phone: *If an employee's tips combined with the employer's direct wages of at least $2.13 an hour do not equal the federal minimum hourly wage, the employer must make up the difference.*

With the information I derived from Managerial Accounting, I was able to calculate that Jennifer was being ripped off by about $2500 a year. I explained this to some of her co-workers as well, and told them of what their boss was doing to them. Of course, I made sure that he was not around first... I realize I'll probably never work for a Big 4 Accounting firm or have a successful Law firm in Birmingham, Nashville, or Atlanta, but do you think that Jennifer and her fellow employees care about that? I doubt it, but hopefully they were able to see some *value* in my *core*.

AUTHOR'S NOTE

Inevitably, when you write a book with a strong religious tone, you open yourself to the charge of being called a hypocrite. Before that accusation is even thrown at me, I admit it, I am one. Often times, I have fallen short of living out The Golden Rule to others.

REFERENCES

Introduction

1. *Holy Bible*. NIV. 1986. Zondervan. Grand Rapids, Michigan. Matthew 7:12 p. 1506
2. "To Kill a Mockingbird" at Fifty. Eileen Reynolds. June 14th, 2010. The New Yorker. http://www.newyorker.com/books/page-turner/to-kill-a-mockingbird-at-fifty
3. http://www.telegraph.co.uk/news/2138827/To-Kill-a-Mockingbird-voted-Greatest-Novel-Of-All-Time.html Urmee Khan. 16 June 2008. To Kill a Mockingbird Voted Greatest Novel of all Time. The Telegraph.
4. *Uncle Tom's Cabin*. Harriet Beecher Stowe. 2001. Modern Library Paperback Edition. Random House: New York.
5. "Robert E. Lee Would Have Despised the Alt-Right March in Charlottesville." John Tures: August 14th, 2017. *Observer*
6. *Lee Considered*. Alan T. Nolan. 1991. United States of America.
7. *Lincoln's Melancholy*. Joshua Wolf Shenk. First Mariner Books. 2006. New York. p. 139
8. "How MLK Day Become a Holiday." Lily Rothman. January 15th, 2015. http://time.com/3661538/mlk-day-reagan-history/ .
9. *First Rate Madness*. Penguin Books. Nassir Ghaemi. 2012. New York.
10. http://www.rutgersprep.org/kendall/books/what_the_dog_saw.html "Notes on *What the Dog Saw* by Malcom Gladwell." 8-6-2017.

Chapter 1

1. – p. 139: *UTC*.
2. *Holy Bible*. P. 1816.
3. p. 200: *To Kill a Mockingbird*: Harper Lee: First Warner Books : 1982. New York.
4. Holy Bible. Luke 6:26. P. 1601
5. "Letter from Robert E. Lee to His Son. Transcribed by Mattie S. Meadows. 1937. http://www.victorianvilla.com/sims-mitchell/local/lee/re/letter/01/
6. P. 201 *TKM*
7. *Mare with Mysteries Robert E. Lee's Other Warhorse: The Lucy Long Story* by Susan Anthony Torbert
8. *Personal Reminiscences, Anecdotes, and Letters of Gen. Robert E. Lee* (1874) by John William Jones, p. 170
9. P.75-76. *TKM.*
10. *Uncle Tom's Cabin*: p.115-21
11. *Holy Bible* Matthew 7:12 p. 1506
12. *Holy Bible* 25:41 p .1542

Chapter 2

1. *TKM*: p. 216-217
2. *The Virginia School Journal* p. 301 Richmond 1904.
3. *TKM* p. 98
4. MLK Jr. in Montgomery Speech, 1957.
5. *Holy Bible* p 1641 Luke 23.34.
6. *TKM p.218*
7. *The Pearl.* John Steinbeck. 1947. Viking Press
8. *UTC* p. 514

9. *Holy Bible* p. 1447 Micah 6:8b
10. *UTC* p. 506-507, 509
11. *UTC* p. 560

Chapter 3

1. *UTC* (350)
2. Jones, E. Stanley. The Christ of the Indian Road, New York: The Abingdon Press,1925. (Page 114)
3. *UTC* – p. 262
4. *Holy Bible.* Acts 2:44 p. 1694
5. *TKM* p.230
6. "Opinion: U.S, Racists Dishonor Robert E. Lee by Association." Edward C. Smith September 7th, 2001. http://news.nationalgeographic.com/news/2001/09/0907_smithgenlee.html
7. "Letter from Robert E. Lee to His Son. Transcribed by Mattie S. Meadows. 1937. http://www.victorianvilla.com/sims-mitchell/local/lee/re/letter/01/
8. *UTC*, p.632
9. *TKM* p.157
10. *A Return to Love: Reflections on the Principles of "A Course in Miracles"*, Ch. 7, Section 3 (1992), p. 190.

Chapter 4

1. *TKM* p.174
2. *TKM* p.58
3. *Holy Bible* Jeremiah 29:11. P.1221
4. *First Rate Madness* p.15
5. *TKM* p.105.

Chapter 5

1. *First Rate Madness* – epigraph
2. *UTC* p.504
3. *UTC* p.245
4. *Holy Bible* Luke 6:26 p.1601
5. unsent letter to Bayard Taylor, June 10, 1878. Published in Mark Twain at Large by Arthur L. Scott
6. *Holy Bible* Matthew 10:29-30 p. 1511-12
7. Letter from Birmingham Jail 16 April 1963
8. Letter from Birmingham Jail 16 April 1963

Chapter 6

9. *Holy Bible page* 1500. Matthew 4: 1-11.
10. *UTC* p. 552
11. Letter from Birmingham Jail 16 April 1963
12. *TKM* p. 215
13. http://www.afi.com/100years/handv.aspx
14. *Holy Bible.* Luke 12:19.
15. *UTC* p.586
16. *Holy Bible* 1503 Matthew 5:43-38
17. *UTC* p.285
18. *Moral Animal* Robert Wright 1994
19. *Holy Bible* 1751. Romans 3:23.

Chapter 7

1. *Holy Bible* 1676. John 14:15.
2. *Holy Bible* 1666. John 10:12.

3. *TKM* Page 20
4. *Holy Bible* 1527. Matthew 18:21-35.
5. *UTC p.* 332-333
6. *TKM.* p. 23-25
7. *UTC.* p. 402

Chapter 8

1. "The Maya Angelou Quote That Will Radically Improve Your Business." Carmen Gallo. May 14th, 2014. https://www.forbes.com/sites/carminegallo/2014/05/31/the-maya-angelou-quote-that-will-radically-improve-your-business/#747ff883118b
2. George Washington Farewell Address: September 19th, 1796.
3. Amelia Rawls. Washington Post. http://www.washingtonpost.com/wp-dyn/content/article/2008/04/30/AR2008043003263.html May 1, 2008.
4. *David and Goliath.* Malcom Gladwell.
5. *Great Gatsby.* F. Scott Fitzgerald.
6. Thomas Paine. *The Crisis.*
7. http://www.cio.com/article/3013221/careers-staffing/how-sap-is-hiring-autistic-adults-for-tech-jobs.html 8/7/2017.
8. *TKM* p.281
9. *Holy Bible.* p. 1025. Proverbs 27:17
10. *UTC* p.292
11. *Holy Bible* p. 1877 Hebrews 12:4-12.
12. *UTC* p.439
13. *UTC* p.310

Chapter 9

1. *UTC* p.560
2. *Holy Bible.* James 2:14-26 p. 1882.
3. *UTC* p. 588-89
4. *UTC* p. 496-497
5. *UTC* p.594
6. *UTC* p. 385
7. *UTC* p. 391
8. *UTC* p. 236
9. *Thinking Fast and Slow.* Daniel Kahneman. Farrar, Straus, and Giroux. New York. 2013. p. 41.
10. *UTC-* p. 407
11. *UTC –* p. 425
12. *UTC –* p.436

Conclusion

1. *TKM –* p. 98
2. *TKM* p. 215

CPSIA information can be obtained
at www.ICGtesting.com
Printed in the USA
LVOW03s1010131117
556087LV00008B/382/P